Beyond Happiness

Beyond Happiness

The Zen Way to
True Contentment

Ezra Bayda

 Shambhala · Boston & London · 2010

SHAMBHALA PUBLICATIONS, INC.
Horticultural Hall
300 Massachusetts Avenue
Boston, Massachusetts 02115
www.shambhala.com

9 8 7 6 5 4 3 2

Printed in the United States of America

⊗ This edition is printed on acid-free paper that meets the American
National Standards Institute z39.48 Standard.
♻ This book was printed on 30% postconsumer recycled paper. For more
information please visit www.shambhala.com.

Distributed in the United States by Random House, Inc.,
and in Canada by Random House of Canada Ltd

Designed by Daniel Urban-Brown

Library of Congress Cataloging-in-Publication Data

Bayda, Ezra.
Beyond happiness: the Zen way to true contentment / Ezra Bayda.—1st ed.
  p.   cm.
ISBN 978-1-59030-825-7 (hardcover: alk. paper)
  1. Religious life—Zen Buddhism. 2. Happiness—Religious aspects—
Zen Buddhism. 3. Zen Buddhism—Doctrines. I. Title.
B9286.2.B39 2010
294.3'442—DC22
2010022472

Contents

Acknowledgments

This is a book about genuine happiness. In the spirit of the topic I've included a number of jokes, based on my view that it's worthwhile to poke little holes in the often-held view that Zen practice and spiritual awakening must be somber and serious activities. In the face of life's difficulties, it's always good to find something to brighten our spirits. Cultivating a sense of humor is actually essential to living from the lightened heart of true contentment. This is particularly true when we acknowledge how easy it is to take ourselves too seriously. Most of the jokes I tell in this book have been adapted from the book *Plato and a Platypus Walk into a Bar . . .* by Thomas Cathcart and Daniel Klein, a book I highly recommend to anyone who wishes to lighten up.

Thanks to the people at Shambhala Publications for their continuing support, specifically to Dave O'Neal, who initially encouraged me to write this book, and to Eden Steinberg, who gently and skillfully helped in clarifying my message.

Thanks to my daughter Jenessa, who has edited all five of my books, always with a perceptive eye for nuance. And finally, I am continuously thankful to my wife and fellow teacher, Elizabeth, not only for her keen insight as an editor but also for her unwavering support and irrepressible good cheer.

Beyond Happiness

Introduction
What Is Happiness?

Many books and articles have been published in the last several years on happiness, most of them promising quick fixes—guarantees to take away our anxiety and depression and replace them with a cheerful outlook. But evidence suggests that since this happiness "boom" began, our levels of anxiety and dis-ease have actually increased. The sense of entitlement that comes with the belief that happiness is our birthright, and the typically Western belief in the quick fix, seems to have led to an even greater sense of disconnectedness.

The Dalai Lama has said that the purpose of human life is to be happy. Philosophers such as Aristotle, St. Augustine, and Pascal have said the same thing. This is certainly a good question to ask ourselves: Is the purpose of human life to be happy? But perhaps we should first ask: What do we mean by happiness?

A while back a fairly new student came to talk to me about his Zen practice. In the middle of our conversation he acknowledged that he really didn't care about being enlightened or anything deeply spiritual—he said he just wanted to be happy. He asked me if, after my years of meditating and teaching Zen, I felt I was truly happy. I answered that yes, I felt genuinely happy, but what I meant by being happy was quite possibly not the same as he might understand it. It was certainly different from the way I used to understand it.

Often, when we're young, we equate happiness with pleasure and sensual enjoyment. As we get older, we may equate it more with security and control—having things like money and good health. We might also equate it with our accomplishments. Or we could equate it with the connection we feel in particular relationships. It's important to realize that all of these aspects or levels of happiness are based, in part, on the external circumstances of our lives. Yet perhaps external circumstances play a smaller role in our happiness than we might believe.

Interestingly, current research has proven this, that external circumstances have a much smaller impact than we may think in determining our happiness. Instead, it appears that each of us is born with a happiness "set point." We are each predisposed to feel a certain level of happiness, and no matter the circumstances of our lives, we tend to return to our set point. You could say that we come out of the womb with our happiness level already set. For example, if we are born with a high set point—naturally upbeat and optimistic—we could get very sick or become paralyzed and still, after a period of adjustment, be just as happy as we were before we got sick or disabled. By contrast, if we are born with a low set point for happiness—with a predisposition for seeing the glass as half empty—we could inherit a million dollars, and even though we might be happy for a while, we would eventually return to our original state of unhappiness.

There is no doubt that external conditions can have some effect within this limited range, but because the range is somewhat fixed, changing our external conditions will not change our degree of happiness all that much. So seeking happiness based solely on externals does not work all that well, as perhaps you have already found out. Besides, even to the degree that externals can, in fact, make us happier, the externals can always change—we can lose our job, or our wealth, or our relationships, or our health. Eventually we have to accept that relying on externals is like building a foundation on sand. This may not be easy to accept, and it may take many disappointments to realize the truth that we can't rely on externals for happiness. But if externals are not the source of happiness, we might wonder, is there anything that can help us become happier?

Discussions about happiness are often imbued with platitudes, such as the illusion that money will bring us happiness. But experience has shown that money does not bring us happiness, except when it lifts us out of poverty. Once we have financial security, which we think should make us happy, we usually get caught in wanting more affluence, in fearing its loss, or in wanting to keep up with our peers—thus, happiness eludes us. The myth that money will bring us happiness is just one among many of our illusions. We need to see how these common misperceptions about happiness keep us stuck in the same endless cycles of discontent.

How about drugs as a source of happiness? Medications such as antidepressants certainly can help make us a little happier, or at least tone down the unhappiness of anxiety and depression. And for those who suffer from severe or chronic depression, they are necessary as a mechanical adjustment to our physiology, much like the use of insulin to control diabetes. But drugs usually have side effects, and we may need increasing doses, so medication has not proven to be a good long-term approach to feeling happier. Besides, drugs do not affect underlying conditions, the very conditions that may be at the root of our unhappiness; so even when they can give us a sense of stability, they still can't give us happiness on a deeper level.

How about psychotherapy as a way to happiness? Therapy can certainly help, especially in getting to know ourselves. But even psychologists will admit that the efficacy of therapy in enabling people to be happy is very limited. Their goal is perhaps more modest—to allow people to feel more adjusted to their lives or, at the very least, to feel less miserable.

How about spiritual practice? Can spiritual practice actually make us happier? There's a study in which participants were asked to listen to a piece of classical music. Half were told to just listen; the other half were told to try to feel happy while listening to the music. The results were quite interesting— the participants who were *trying* to be happy reported being much less so than those who were just listening. Why? Because in trying to be happy they were caught in their heads, whereas simply being present with the music allowed the other participants to experience the genuine happiness of "just being there," not trying to be or to feel different.

I don't know if there are many scientific studies on this, but my own observation and personal experience indicate that people who devote sufficient time to meditation and to trying to live in a way that is more awake generally experience increasing happiness in their lives. This has certainly been true for me, especially given the fact that I was born with a fairly low set point for happiness. My viewpoint for years, based in a pervasive and deeply seated feeling of anxiety, could have been summed up in the words, "Life is too hard—I can't do it." Yet I no longer believe these words, nor do I experience that ongoing anxious quiver in my being. In fact, even when I experienced a very long period of physical illness, punctuated by weeks on end of nausea and severe discomfort, I learned that it was possible to experience true contentment in the midst of it.

Yet, interestingly, in spiritual practice, happiness is not the goal. When we make happiness the goal, it normally eludes us, as it did with the people trying to feel happy while listening to music. Happiness is not so much a feeling to be attained as it is a by-product of how we live.

This leads back to the question: What do we actually mean

by happiness? The dictionary describes happiness as a state characterized by delight or contentment—the emotional feeling that life is good. It is almost always associated with getting the good stuff, like pleasure, or getting the things we want, like financial security or good health or satisfying relationships. This version of happiness—our everyday personal happiness—is based in part on two things over which we have little control: first, on our set point or genetic predisposition toward happiness, and second, on the ever-changing ups and downs of our particular life circumstances. When people talk about happiness they are usually referring to this version of everyday personal happiness.

But there is another kind of happiness that goes beyond personal happiness, one not based on either our personal predispositions or ephemeral external conditions. This is the deeper, more genuine experience of true contentment—of being fundamentally okay with life as it is, no longer being attached to our demand that life be a particular way. This deeper happiness of equanimity is the natural state of our being when our self-centered thinking and emotions no longer get in the way. In this sense, although this experience of happiness has no external cause, it can still be cultivated by working with all the things that block its natural occurrence. As we get to know ourselves, and begin to see all the ways we thwart our natural happiness—our sense of entitlement, our wallowing in the past or worrying about the future, our disconnecting emotions, our deeply conditioned behaviors, our attachments—we can learn what it takes to cultivate this more genuine state of true contentment.

The whole idea of being happy is often muddied by the fact that thoughts about happiness frequently switch back and forth between the everyday or ephemeral happiness, which is based on externals, and the deeper kind of happiness that comes when we stop trying to make life and ourselves different. We have to be clear about which kind of happiness we're talking about, because they are two very different things. Yet, even though they are different, the pleasantness of ephemeral happiness can certainly be included within the deeper, lasting experience of happiness.

The basic teaching underlying every religion and every spiritual path is that it's possible to experience fundamental happiness, but that this happiness comes from the inside; it cannot depend on our external life circumstances. Nor can it depend on simply feeling good emotionally. Many things can result in pleasurable or positive feelings, which we normally equate with being happy. But this is personal happiness, not the deeper sense of well-being that is not dependent on whether or not we feel good in the normal sense. For example, many things make me feel personally happy, such as playing my conga drums, playing basketball, or riding the ocean waves on my boogie board. Sometimes when I'm in the ocean I feel positively exhilarated, and there's certainly nothing wrong with this, nor can I deny that this form of happiness is real. Similarly, when I play my drums I sometimes get into that state known as the zone, where I'm totally absorbed in the activity, with no sense of "me" playing. This state of absorption is quite nice, and we may feel very happy when in it—but eventually, it will pass. My point is that absorption is not the same as the deeper sense of happiness that's possible.

So, although absorption, or being in the zone, can often feel quite good, pursuing these experiences to find happiness is often a detour off the path toward true contentment. Whenever we seek special experiences to bring us happiness we are caught in striving, in the self-centered pursuit to feel a particular way. This is guaranteed to undermine any aspiration to realize our true nature, which is ultimately the source of the deeper equanimity of genuine happiness.

Put in different words: there is no single or fixed path to happiness, nor does happiness have to look any particular way.

There is, however, something in each of us that longs to connect with what is most real. We may easily get sidetracked from this quest with promises or quick formulas to bring us happiness—formulas that tell us we can be happy if we do this or that. But formulas for happiness can only give us superficial fixes; they don't and can't deal with the complexity of human emotion and behavior.

In short, happiness doesn't come from making happiness the goal—it comes from being able to appreciate the journey, particularly the present-moment experience of our life. To "enjoy the ride" doesn't mean we're going to get somewhere, or get something, or become someone else; it means we're curious about what our life is and able to appreciate it—even the most difficult, unpleasant, unwanted aspects of it. In this sense, we can say that true happiness is more about being present, being awake, being open, than it is about being happy in the Hollywood sense of being merry and cheerful.

Genuine happiness is not exhilaration; it's not a rush of sensual pleasure or being cheerful all the time. These aspects can be included, but genuine happiness at its core boils down to the willingness to acknowledge the painful aspects of life right alongside all the parts we deem "good" or "happy." In fact, an integral part of genuine happiness is the willingness to open to the feelings and experiences we would not normally associate with happiness. Sadness, for example, cannot be denied as a basic human experience. To try to prematurely let go of sadness denies us the possibility of surrendering to it, where we can learn to experience true equanimity even within the sadness.

It may be difficult to understand how it is possible to experience happiness in light of the undeniable and ongoing suffering in the world. For example, when we open our hearts and minds to what is actually going on, how do we respond to the fact that we're not taking care of the planet or providing for the twenty-four thousand people who die every single day from hunger—three-quarters of them being children under the age of five? How do we reconcile facts like these with living a happy life, with being able to appreciate the beauty of the mockingbird singing with abandon or the majesty and wonder of the ocean? This is the crux of the human dilemma—abiding in the paradox that includes both the bleakness and the wonder. Although it may at times be very difficult to find this balance, it is, in fact, possible. Moreover, the compassion and loving-kindness that develop from being able to face life's pains can lead to an even greater sense of equanimity.

The Dalai Lama would most likely agree with this, since he also says that the greatest happiness comes from the cultivation of compassion and loving-kindness—not from self-centered pursuits. Studies bear this out; it's been found that people who live a life based in giving or service to others are generally happier than other people. It also helps to cultivate perspective and a sense of humor. After all, everything is relative, depending on our perspective. We're reminded of this by the story of the snail who was mugged by a turtle. When asked what happened, the snail replied, "I don't know—it all happened so fast."

Some of us may still hope that one great experience, like an enlightenment or mystical experience, will promote lasting happiness. But even though such experiences can show us possibilities, and in some ways help change our viewpoint, they rarely have a lasting impact on our behavior. Take the example of the many thousands of people who go to workshops or find the latest guru. They may have some dramatic insights or become deeply inspired, but after a few weeks or months there is often not even a residue of that insight or inspiration. And the reason for this is clear—we can't just change the mind without addressing the deeply seated conditioning in the body.

This is also why moral training doesn't really work in making us happier. Even though we can firmly know what is the "right" behavior—say, to refrain from anger or inappropriate desire—our bodies, with their deeply conditioned emotional history, have another view, one that is often more compelling than a primarily mental, moral dictate.

So instead of trying to stamp out behaviors we don't like, the path to true happiness requires our openhearted attention to the very things that seem to block our way to it—especially to all the things we are most inclined to run from, reject, change, or be rid of. Thus, when we're unhappy, rather than making happiness our goal, we must try instead to see that *whatever* is on our plate is our opportunity to work with and free ourselves from what gets in the way of happiness.

In fact, in any given moment we can ask ourselves three questions that will put us on the direct path to cultivating the genuine happiness of true contentment. The first: Am I truly happy right now? The second: If not, what blocks it? And the third: Can I surrender to what is? Later, we'll explore the power of working with these three questions as one approach to cultivating the roots of happiness. I've found that these three questions alone, when used in a particular way, can make tremendous inroads in unlocking the mystery of why genuine happiness seems to elude us. In addition, we'll explore what nourishes the roots of happiness directly—not through *trying* to be happy but through cultivating the generosity of the heart, which includes the essential qualities of gratitude and forgiveness.

It's presumptuous to assume there is an easy formula to attain happiness. If there were some easy formula it would have been discovered by now. As Woody Allen once said, "I'm astounded by people who want to 'know' the universe when it's hard enough to find your way around Chinatown." However, if you follow the guidelines suggested in this book with patience and perseverance, you can learn two essential things: first, how to see and work with what blocks happiness;

and second, how to water the roots of happiness directly. This starts with cultivating the ability to be truly present to our life, and eventually it includes learning to actually live from the generosity of the awakened heart.

Part One

What Blocks Happiness?

1

Entitlement

Learning to live from genuine happiness requires first seeing what blocks it. One of the major blocks is our deeply rooted sense of entitlement. In fact, this is a big part of the "problem" of happiness: we firmly believe that we *should* be happy. We think it's our right, and consequently, we feel entitled to it, even if we're not clear what happiness is, except to feel good. This expectation can have many faces. For example, we often feel entitled to good health, expecting that we can and should be able to stay youthful and physically fit. When life comes along to greet us with illness or injury we can easily sink into a stupor of frustration and even despair. Sometimes just getting a cold will trigger our anxieties over losing control and feeling powerless. This sense of entitlement—which basically says that life should go the way we want and expect it to go—even tells us we shouldn't have to experience discomfort. Then, when we do experience discomfort, we feel that something is wrong; we might get angry and feel it's unfair, or we may feel sorry for ourselves.

Having a sense of entitlement also guarantees that we will eventually feel like a victim. When we don't get what we firmly believe is rightfully ours, namely happiness, we'll experience the emotional discord of discouragement. And in feeding the negative feelings of being slighted or wronged, we actually increase our unhappiness. Still, it isn't easy to give up the entitled belief that we should be happy; the belief that we deserve all of the good stuff is deeply ingrained in our thinking. Unfortunately we can't be happy just because we want to be. Nor can we just act happy—say, by smiling—and expect to *be* happy, except in the most superficial way. If we want to be happy we have to acknowledge that, yes, we want to be happy but that, no, most of the time, we're not; and in fact, all of the things that are supposed to make us happy—such as accomplishments, respect, love, sex, money, and praise—only give us happiness in ephemeral doses, not in the deep or lasting way that we truly desire.

If Only

Along with our sense of entitlement, we have many specific ideas and expectations about what will make us feel happy. "If only I had the right partner I'd be happy." "If only I had a better job, or more money, I'd no longer be anxious." "If only I had a better body I'd be content." The one thing all of our "if onlies" have in common is an underlying unwillingness to actually be with the present-moment circumstances of our life. Instead, we choose to live in endorphin-producing fantasies about the future. From one point of view this is understandable, in that it's certainly more comfortable to hold onto our expectations of a different and better reality than it is to be with what is. Yet, where does this leave us? It leaves us living a life that is neither real nor satisfying.

But remember, the path to genuine happiness entails first recognizing what blocks it. We have to clearly acknowledge our many "if onlies," our subtle demands that life be different from what it is. Recognizing our "if only" attitude toward life is the first step in diminishing our sense of entitlement. Then we can begin to face the reality that is right in front of us. We may not want to face this reality, and we may not like it when we do, but as we'll learn later, being fully present with what is can open doorways into a reality that we perhaps didn't even know was possible—the reality of genuine happiness. But first we have to do the work of objectively observing and recognizing where we're stuck holding on to entitlement and demands toward life.

It's also very common to take our "if only" mind directly into our spiritual practice. For example, "If only I had an enlightenment experience, then I would be happy and at peace." Or, "If only I could go on more meditation retreats, I would really make some progress." Or how many of us still have the assumption that meditation is supposed to make us feel good? If this is our entitlement, what will happen when we don't feel good? Aren't we bound to fall into disappointment or self-judgment—or even believe that practice is defective?

The underlying assumption here is that if we practice long enough and hard enough, our suffering will go away. But even after years of sincere efforts, our discomforts may certainly remain—and this is where we get stuck, because our sense of entitlement tells us that all the bad stuff *should* go away. This deeply held belief, that practice will take away our suffering, can take many forms—the longing for comfort, calmness, freedom from fear, or some vague notion of enlightenment. These longings may motivate us for many years; after all, don't all of us want to be free of the anxious quiver of being at our core? But ironically, it's only as we see what practice is *not* that we can begin to see what practice actually is. And if we're fortunate, we may begin to see through our illusions of entitlement.

Our Illusions

So what is the source of this entitlement? It comes from the ego, the small mind that is trying to control its world, trying to have life on its own terms. We all know the top hit of the ego's silent soundtrack—"If I do this I'll feel better." Seeing through our own particular version of this is part of the process of waking up. Again, the essence of this entitlement is the assumption that we can make ourselves, and life, be the way we want them to be. But this can only bring disappointment. Why? Because no matter what we do, there's no way that we can guarantee a life that is free of problems.

Along with our sense of entitlement, we often live with many illusions about ourselves and about how life is supposed to be. For example, we may like to read and talk about spiritual practice, and we may see ourselves as altruistic, just wanting to live a good life and help others. But our ability to deceive ourselves is sometimes quite remarkable. In wanting to see ourselves as caring about the welfare of others, we may totally ignore our self-centeredness. However, sooner or later we'll come to the place where real efforts are required—beyond reading and talking—and we may see how unwilling we are to pay the price of practice.

There was a man who thought he wanted to better humanity. When he would read the newspapers or listen to the news he would get depressed about the suffering in the world, but he didn't know where to start. Nonetheless, he firmly believed it was his calling to serve. One day when he was out shopping, he walked into a store and was surprised to find the Buddha standing behind the counter. He was certain it was the Buddha, but just to be sure he asked him, "Excuse me, are you the Buddha?" The Buddha answered, "Yes, this is my store. We sell anything you want. What do you want?" The man answered, "I don't know." The Buddha then said, "Feel free to look around, make a list of whatever you see that you want, and then come back and let me know."

The man walked up and down the aisles, looking at what was available in this unusual store: clean air, an end to war, peaceful cooperation between countries, the eradication of racial and gender prejudice, loving-kindness, forgiveness, and on and on.

He made a long list of everything he wanted and then came back to give the Buddha his list. The Buddha looked at it and smiled, and then went below the counter and picked out a bunch of little packets. The man asked, "What are these?" The Buddha replied, "These are seed packets." The man said, "But what about all the things I really want?" The Buddha smiled again and said, "These are the things you asked for, in seed form. You can plant them. You cultivate them and nurture their growth, and someone else reaps the benefits." "Oh, in that case I'll pass," the man said and left the store without buying anything.

Part of the path toward genuine happiness is recognizing where we live out of illusions, especially about ourselves. Being honest with ourselves means acknowledging where we hold onto false pictures of who we are. Just like our sense of entitlement, which demands that life be other than it is, our false self-images also deny reality. But facing what is, as it is, is a direct step toward the deeper reality that we aspire to. The man in this story had the opportunity to look right in the mirror of reality, and in clearly seeing his unwillingness to pay the price of a life of service, he would no longer be stuck in having to maintain a false ideal of who he was supposed to be. The possibility for a more genuine life, a life of increasing happiness, opens as we look honestly at our deeply embedded beliefs, especially our entitlement and our illusions.

Our beliefs and illusions about life are many and varied. Here are a few of the more common ones:

"Life should be fair." Almost everyone sustains this belief on a fundamental level.

"People should be reasonable." In spite of all the evidence to the contrary, we still hang on to this expectation.

"Governments (and politicians) should be honest." We may think we don't believe this, but if we get self-righteously angry when political dishonesty becomes evident, it means we still hold to that belief.

"Spiritual leaders should never cause harm." Even after the many instances of transgressions on the part of spiritual leaders and teachers, this is a hard one to give up, because we want so much for it to be true. Spiritual leaders do have a mandate to be trustworthy; however, whenever we have a strong emotional reaction to something a teacher does, it is a red flag that there is a belief on board, whether we're aware of it or not.

One way to become aware of our specific beliefs and fantasies about life is to ask ourselves the following question whenever we're feeling low: "How do I think it's supposed to be?" This question will usually point us directly to our specific expectation or entitlement.

The point in seeing through these entitled beliefs about how things should be is not to become cynical. After all, cynical beliefs like "life is cruel" or "people can't be trusted" are also just beliefs, arising from disappointments that remain unhealed. The point is to cease living out of *any* sense of entitlement, because every entitlement we hold to, every mental picture we have of how life is supposed to be, blocks our ability to be truly present with what is.

Perhaps the most basic belief underlying all of our feelings of entitlement, our "if onlies," and even our illusions, is the belief that life should please us, that life should be comfortable. All of our resistance to life is rooted in our wanting life to be pleasing, comfortable, and safe. When life doesn't give us what we want—the job that isn't satisfying, the relationship that isn't quite working, the body that ages or breaks down—we resist. Our resistance can manifest as anger, or fear, or self-pity, or depression, but whatever form it takes, it blocks our ability to experience true contentment. We see our discomfort as the problem: yet it's the *belief* that we can't be happy if we're uncomfortable that is much more of a problem than the discomfort itself. One of the most freeing discoveries of an awareness practice is when we realize firsthand that we can, in fact, experience equanimity even in the midst of discomfort.

Recently my wife, Elizabeth, and I went to Paris, and on our first day there I started feeling pretty flu-ish, with a bad sore throat. When we went out for a walk, it started raining, and by the time we sat down to rest in Notre Dame Cathedral, I was feeling pretty crummy, and it had all the makings of A Miserable Moment.

So I asked myself: What's blocking happiness right now? And the answer was obvious. It was the story of the future—about how I wouldn't be able to enjoy our time in Paris if I was sick, about how it might rain for four days, and so forth. But dropping the story of the future, just staying with the actual physical experience of the present moment, the potentially miserable moment became an experience of just mildly unpleasant physical sensations. But more than that, I realized that the present moment included sitting next to Elizabeth in one of the most beautiful churches in the world. As I surrendered to the experience—sore throat and all—the experience was one of a deep and quiet joy, despite not feeling well.

What was required was two things: first, seeing that I was caught in my mental picture of how life was supposed to be; and second, being able to surrender into the very specific physical experience of the present moment. This is a key point that will be emphasized over and over—getting out of the head and into the body. Awareness, and the appreciation and happiness that can come with awareness, doesn't often happen without the intention to be more awake. Awareness allows us to see where we're stuck, where we're holding onto beliefs or feelings of entitlement. Seeing these blockages is the first step in finding the way to true contentment, of moving beyond the smaller, ephemeral experience of personal happiness.

2
The Thinking Mind

Two friends are making breakfast. One of them, while buttering his toast, says, "Have you ever noticed that when you drop your toast on the floor it always lands butter-side down?" The other replies, "I don't think that's true. I think it probably just seems that way because you remember the mess." The first one then says, "Okay—watch this," and lets the toast fall. When it lands butter-side up, the second one says, "See, I told you it doesn't always happen." The first one responds, "No, I know what happened. I just buttered the wrong side."

This may sound silly, but is it really any sillier than the more serious thoughts we entertain and often believe wholeheartedly as the truth? While this man's belief about dropping toast doesn't cause any harm, many of the thoughts we cling to do—both to ourselves and to others. In fact, what blocks genuine happiness the most is being caught in the thinking mind—lamenting about the past or worrying about the future. Or, as in the man's belief about the buttered toast, we can see how our beliefs act like radar: what we perceive is determined by what we're believing and looking for. Living in our heads, the ground of all our judgments, fears, and limiting beliefs, creates a self-centered narrowness and is a prescription for unhappiness.

It is quite interesting to begin observing all the ways we get caught in the thinking mind. For example, many people spend a lot of time planning. There's nothing wrong with planning when a situation requires it, but simple observation shows us that we're often *lost* in planning without even knowing it. Nor do we realize that planning is often just an attempt to maintain control. Analysis can be similar: sometimes analyzing is the appropriate response to a situation, but most of the time it's our need for control that drives us to try to figure everything out, even to the point of analyzing people or situations obsessively. Although neither planning nor analyzing is blatantly harmful, how can we possibly experience genuine happiness when we're caught in either? It's useful to occasionally ask yourself the question "Am I truly happy right now?" And if the answer is "no," which it will most often be if you're honest, you can then ask, What blocks happiness? When you experience what it feels like to be caught in the narrow world of thinking, it becomes obvious how both planning and analyzing block the experience of true contentment.

The same is true for other ways we get caught in the thinking mind, like fantasizing, which is often a way of avoiding something unpleasant in the present. Others have imaginary conversations, in order to view themselves in a positive light or as a way to make their case. And some spend hours in random daydreams, totally lost to the present. Again, even though none of these tendencies are particularly harmful, none ultimately makes us happier, except in the most superficial, temporary way.

Other forms of thinking are more pernicious. Blaming, in particular, is a way of poisoning our lives, and when the blaming thoughts come out of our mouths, or manifest outwardly via body language, they also poison others. Lamenting about the past and worrying about the future are also harmful, in that they tend to feed and solidify a gloomy and narrow experience of reality. We all do this to some extent, but for some it becomes almost an addiction. For instance, worrying about the future, left unchecked, can turn into full-blown catastrophizing, where everything seems dark and unworkable. In addition, it can seem *real*, and cause us unnecessary distress over a situation that isn't even happening, and that may, in fact, never happen.

Recognizing the First and Second Arrows

Buddha once said that if we're hit by an arrow it will surely hurt, but if we're hit by a second arrow in the same spot it will hurt much more. This may sound like common sense, but if we use the second arrow as an analogy to help clarify the harmful qualities of the thinking mind, its meaning deepens and becomes more useful. For example, if we get a headache, there's no doubt it can be somewhat painful. But if we have the thought, "This is terrible" or "Why is this happening to me?" it's like being hit by a second arrow, and it intensifies the physical pain. As we observe ourselves, we'll see that we shoot ourselves with second arrows quite regularly, even though we're normally not aware that we're doing this. Why? Because we accept our thoughts and judgments as the unquestioned truth. How many times have you thought, "This isn't fair," without even questioning whether or not the thought was true? Or after making a mistake, which we can call the first arrow, we add the second-arrow thought, "I can't do anything right."

Sometimes our thoughts can even serve as the first arrow. Last year I was scheduled for an invasive medical procedure. I didn't have any pain, or even mild discomfort, but the procedure was strongly recommended as a precautionary diagnostic. A few days before the procedure, my mind began entertaining the usual suspects: "I don't want to do this!" "What if it's painful?" And so on. I could feel the level of anxiety rising with each thought. However, when I asked myself the question

"What is blocking happiness right now?" it was obvious I was shooting myself unnecessarily (and repeatedly) with arrows; that is, my indulgence of thoughts about the future, based in the fear of the unknown, had taken over. But then I remembered one of my favorite mantras: Not Happening Now! It became obvious that there was no pain or physical discomfort in the present, except what was generated by my first-arrow thoughts. Seeing this whole dynamic clearly allowed the anxiety to dissipate, but we should never underestimate the power of the thinking mind to undermine happiness.

It's a given that the thinking mind will think. The goal is *not* to stop our thoughts. Nor is it to try to change them. Although changing our attitudes can be helpful in giving us relief in the short run, such changes don't go deep enough to be of lasting significance. Our attempt to change our mind with better thoughts only leads to further disappointment or distress. As with affirmations, changing our attitudes works primarily on the mental realm; but real change must also address the deeply seated conditioning in the body, because our thoughts are inextricably connected to the physical body—where our memories, beliefs, and fears are stored, on a cellular level. Only as we observe our thoughts with precision will we begin to see how related they are to how we feel.

The question might arise: If we're not trying to stop or change our thoughts, what can we do so that they no longer block our ability to be happy? The answer is twofold. First, through self-observation, we must see our thoughts clearly. This is not analysis! It is simply observation, and to make the observation process as objective as possible, it's useful to label or name the thoughts that arise. For example, with my medical procedure, I would label the thought by saying, "Believing the thought *I don't want to do this*" or "Believing the thought *It's going to be too painful.*" This labeling process helps us become less invested in or identified with the thoughts. It also helps distinguish or separate the *belief* from reality.

The second step, after we have clearly named our thoughts, is to bring awareness to the specific experience in the physical body and to stay with it long enough to actually feel it. Again, the goal is *not* to change or get rid of anything, but rather simply to observe and experience whatever arises. For example, with the thought "I don't want to do this," there was the distinct feeling of queasiness in my abdomen. Normally, we wouldn't want to stay with this feeling. In fact, we rarely want to stay with any feeling that's unpleasant; but in the end, the harder we resist, the stronger our unwanted feelings become.

This is a very worthwhile process to experiment with— first labeling the thought and second staying with the feeling in the body. In my example, doing this two-part process allowed the anxiety to dissolve in a fairly short period of time. However, it's important to note that it dissolved *not* because I tried to make it go away but rather because I stopped resisting and instead opened to the purely physical experience of what was happening, minus all my beliefs about it. Granted, sometimes our most deeply conditioned beliefs may require more work before they dissipate, but if we don't do this work our thoughts will continue to dictate how we feel and act.

Judgments

Another aspect of the thinking mind, and without doubt the most pernicious, is our tendency to judge. Judgment of others undermines our genuine wish to be happy because it automatically separates us from those we judge. This is particularly true with our critical judgments, where we place ourselves above another by putting them down. And as with much of the activity of the thinking mind, we rarely question the truth of our judgments. We simply believe they are The Truth.

In fact, we have so many unquestioned judgments about others that we can hardly see ourselves. There's a joke about a man who was pretty critical of his wife. He knew she was sensitive to his criticism, so he was trying to be careful. But nonetheless, her faults really bugged him! At one point, he started to notice how she was hard of hearing, but he wasn't sure what to say, so he went to the doctor to ask what to do. The doctor suggested that he try a test: stand where she can't see him and ask a question, first from twenty feet away, then from ten, then from very close to her. He went home, and while she was facing the kitchen sink, from across the room he asked, "What's for dinner?" He didn't hear an answer, so he moved closer and asked again, "What's for dinner?" When there was still no answer, he began to have some really strong judgments about her loss of hearing. Finally, and with great frustration, he walked up right behind her and asked again, "What's for dinner?" His wife turned around and said, "For the third time, chicken!"

Our judgments of others are bad enough, but judgments about ourselves often do even more harm. In fact, one of the biggest obstacles to happiness is our relentless self-judgment, particularly the negative belief that we are essentially flawed or lacking in some way. We all live in the prison of our self-images of how we should be, and we constantly judge ourselves as not measuring up to these images we have of ourselves. As a consequence, we berate ourselves mercilessly. Our negative self-judgments have many flavors—feeling unworthy, stupid, incompetent, unappealing, or, more generically, that we're simply not enough. Sometimes the self-judgment is even harsher—feeling like we're no one, or even like we're a pariah. The point is, in every case, we're caught in the narrow, inaccurate confines of the thinking mind, believing these judgments as the absolute truth. By doing so, we perpetuate our own suffering, shooting ourselves over and over again with arrows. The cycle is vicious and relentless.

Our negative self-judgments are not always on the surface of the mind. Yet they're often at work, impacting the way we relate to the world. In a way, they're like the background operating system programs on our computers, running continuously and inexorably behind the scene. And the one thing the various flavors of our self-judgments have in common is the basic message that "I am bad." We may never say these exact words to ourselves, and the message may be buried in the background, but as we observe ourselves, we will become increasingly aware of its imprint on how we live. In some of us, this message manifests through trying harder to measure up; in others, it comes through in hiding to avoid failure; and for many, it surfaces through finding distractions, ways of numbing ourselves from the pain of holding on to our beliefs.

We may go to extremes to avoid the pain of our self-judgments. In the novel *The Reader*, one of the main characters is a woman who was once a guard at a Nazi concentration camp. Although quite intelligent, she couldn't read or write, and she was so ashamed of being illiterate that she hid it from everyone. Her negative self-judgment was so strong that she wouldn't admit her illiteracy even when her silence meant she would receive a very long prison sentence.

Our self-judgments are often one of the most elusive aspects of the thinking mind and also one of the last things we want to deal with. But if we can get into the habit of asking ourselves the question "Am I truly happy right now?" and following it with the question "What blocks happiness?" we may see the extent to which our happiness is impeded by our negative beliefs about ourselves.

As with our other believed thoughts, we must first observe them with objectivity, labeling them for added clarity: "Believing the thought *I'll never measure up*" or "Believing the thought *I'm unworthy of love.*" We may have to name our believed thoughts in this way a hundred times, but sooner or later our investment in them will diminish. This process of labeling brings not only objectivity but also the quality of mercy—which is the exact opposite of self-judgment—in that the increased objectivity allows us to see and relate to ourselves with more benign tolerance.

next step is to feel the contraction in the thought-body
ted with this belief. What does it feel like, physically,
e believe this thought? Is there a specific feeling in the
body that accompanies our negative self-judgments? If we observe closely, the answer will be yes. This sensation is the feeling
that accompanies the fear that arises from deep in our conditioning—the fear that we're not worthy or not enough—and
the feeling is not a good one. Instinctively we will want to turn
away from it, because we tend to want to avoid discomfort in
any form. But being fully present with this discomfort will often diminish it to the extent that it's no longer problematic.
Again, the objective is not to change or get rid of anything but
to just observe and feel, as objectively as possible, what is happening *right now*—not "why," but simply "what." If we can do
this, the self-judgments may still arise, but we will no longer
believe them as The Truth. I'm not asking you to believe this on
faith. If you sincerely want to live a happier life, you might try
this and verify for yourself what is possible.

Why don't we bring awareness to the beliefs of the thinking
mind more often, since it's so obvious that these beliefs block
happiness? The answer is that the state of waking sleep—in
which we're not aware of what we're thinking or feeling—is
our default setting as human beings. As we observe ourselves
with honesty, we'll see the extent to which we're lost in our
thoughts and feelings, as well as in most of our activities. In
fact, we're rarely truly present, except in brief moments. However, just because the state of unawareness is our default setting doesn't mean it's our permanent setting. It's possible, with
intention and perseverance, to counter the power of waking
sleep, and, as a start, the two practices of observing the mind
and feeling into the physicality of the thought-body can help
us to cultivate a life that is more awake and more aware, and
ultimately more satisfying and happy.

It's possible to observe the mind and feel the body at any
time during the day. You don't need to be meditating or off

by yourself or even in a quiet place. You can take a pause in time anytime—at work, while driving, during meals, and so on. For the duration of just three breaths, simply be present, refraining from engaging in the thinking mind. One particularly fruitful time to step outside of the thinking mind is while you're taking a walk. If you focus some of your awareness on listening to the sounds around you or feeling your feet on the ground, you can more easily observe the mind without getting hooked by the thoughts. Try this when you have to walk a short distance—for example, when you're doing an errand. Instead of the mind being all over the place, which is where it usually is, you will glimpse the possibility of living differently. When walking by a tree, you may actually see and appreciate it, rather than just seeing it through the mental screen of your thoughts—or not at all.

Remember, it's a given that the mind will ceaselessly generate thoughts. With each believed thought we filter and chop up reality, and we end up living in a thought-based world that is neither real nor satisfying. But as we begin to watch the mind—not trying to stop the thinking, but just observing it and feeling how it impacts the body—it is possible to begin to experience an underlying awareness. This wordless sense of presence, which we'll talk about in detail later, is the experience of being, or "hereness." Just as the thinking mind is the seat of self-centeredness and often of our unhappiness, this underlying awareness is one of the sources of our fundamental happiness. But to cultivate this awareness and to live a genuinely happy life, we have to start by uncovering and working with the thoughts that block it.

3

Caught in Emotions

When we observe what blocks happiness within ourselves, we will undoubtedly see the powerful impact of being caught in our emotions, particularly in anger, fear, and despair. We can see and feel how they cut us off from living from our true openhearted nature, which is the ultimate source of fundamental happiness. Anger, for example, is rooted in aversion to life, and it separates us from others. Fear is also a separating emotion, in that it narrows our life down to a protected cocoon world. And despair or depression disconnects us not only from others but also from ourselves. When we're caught in these emotions, we are disconnected from our own hearts. So how can we expect to be happy when we spend so much of our life caught in our emotional reactions? Anger, fear, and depression are just the main suspects—there is also self-doubt, which makes our world small and grim; confusion, which can paralyze us; self-pity, which leaves us feeling victimized; and resentment, which hardens the heart and prevents any chance of genuine happiness.

These separating emotions also deplete our essential life energy. For example, when we express our anger, we squander our life force. I'm not just talking about overt, explosive bursts of rage. We also waste energy in more subtle ways throughout the day—for example, when we express irritability, impatience, passive aggression, and self-righteousness, all of which are forms of anger. Similarly, when we're caught in anxiety and fear, our natural flow of life energy is constricted—a classic case of feeling stuck. And with depression, where we're basically pressing down the emotions that we don't want to feel, such as anger or hurt or fear, we are literally cutting off our life force. That is why, when depressed, we feel so lacking in energy.

Paradoxically, even though these separating emotions squander our energy and also contribute enormously to our unhappiness, we often don't want to give them up. In our misguided quest for personal happiness (in contrast to deeper or more genuine happiness), we still believe that these emotions will somehow serve us. For example, in spite of all the evidence to the contrary, we continue to believe that anger will help protect us and empower us to get what we want. We blame, we confront, we sulk, much like little children who cry louder and louder, thinking this will get them what they want. And we *believe* our thoughts: "If I could just get her to change, then things would be okay." But we rarely get our desired result, and in the meantime, we remain stuck in the closed heart of anger.

With fear, we accept the false sense of safety that comes when we listen to its voice, which tells us to turn away from whatever we perceive as dangerous. But dangerous to whom? Isn't it just to the small mind that wants to stay in the comfort of the familiar? Fear tells us that something is wrong, but when we believe in and indulge this voice, we remain stuck in the narrow, protected cocoon world that fear creates. This is why fear is one of the major blocks to genuine happiness—not just because it feels bad in the moment, but because, under the guise of protecting us and keeping us safe, it prevents us from opening into life. It's ironic how strongly we cling to the belief that avoiding our fears can bring us happiness, because the exact opposite is true. When we imagine the fearful thing we want to avoid, it makes us truly miserable in the present, whereas being able to surrender to our fears (which we'll discuss in detail later) allows our fears to gradually dissipate.

Depression is also a distorted way of trying to feel happy, since it dulls the emotions that we believe will make us unhappy, like hurt and fear. Even though we may think we don't want to be depressed, there's another part of us that fears the discomfort of our buried feelings even more. We don't realize that the feelings themselves are not nearly as problematic as the walls that we erect to protect ourselves—walls that leave us disabled, accepting emotional numbness as a substitute for living. As long as we stay caught in depression, we close off the possibility of opening into life or experiencing the genuine happiness that comes from directly engaging our emotions— including the very emotions we don't want to feel, along with those we enjoy.

These disconnecting emotions of anger, fear, and despair sustain our familiar ways of trying to maintain control. Even when the emotions feel bad, we fear the groundlessness of the unfamiliar even more. In fact, surrendering into groundlessness is perhaps the thing we least want to do. There's a story about a man who falls into a deep well, and on the way down he grabs onto a branch. He's holding onto the branch for dear life, and he yells out, "Help! Is there anyone who can help me?" When he looks up he doesn't see anyone—he only sees the sky. And then the sky miraculously opens up; there is a big flash of light, and the man hears a booming voice say, "I am the Lord and I am here to help you. Let go of the branch and I will save you." The man hesitates for a few moments and then yells out, "Is there anybody else up there who can help me?"

Can we acknowledge that as much as we believe we want happiness, we're often unwilling to pay the price? We say we want to be happy, yet rarely does a day go by that we don't indulge in these disconnecting emotions. We may make occasional efforts to overcome our anger and our fears, but much more frequently we continue feeding them. How can we reconcile our stated wish to be happy with the undeniable fact that we hold on to the very emotions that make us most unhappy?

A student recently asked, "Why do I hold onto blaming and anger when it makes me so unhappy?" I answered that it was most likely because she was still able to enjoy the false sense of being right. In my first marriage, for instance, even though I hated the periods when my former wife and I would engage in power struggles, where we both insisted on being right, I was nonetheless unwilling to stop. The fact is, I really believed I was in the right; and we would often rather feel like we're right than be happy, because we like the juiciness and the false sense of power that accompany our self-righteousness. But like all of the disconnecting emotions, it leaves us with the unsatisfying feeling of being separate.

The Gift of Remorse

We all build walls to protect ourselves from pain; however, in erecting these walls we create a self-imposed prison of separation, cutting ourselves off from others. Unless we can drop the walls of protection we will continue to experience the unhappiness of feeling separate. As the walls slowly come down, however, we can increasingly experience the genuine happiness of being connected to ourselves, to others, and to life itself. But for this to happen, we first have to experience the genuine remorse of living disconnected from ourselves, disconnected from the heart. This feeling of remorse, which is what finally helped me disengage from the struggles with my former wife, is different from guilt; guilt is just another subtle form of anger, directed at ourselves. Remorse, on the other hand, is not based in thoughts or in moral dictates about how we're supposed to be; it's an awareness of the actual ache of living disconnected from the heart. When we feel remorse on this level, we will more likely be motivated to do what is necessary to move out of our conditioned stuckness.

As a hospice volunteer, I spend a few hours a week with patients who are close to death. When I first began visiting patients, I sometimes had anxiety and self-doubt about who I was supposed to be and what specifically I was supposed to do when I was with them. One time I had a patient who was caught in his own disabling emotions, unable to reach out to anyone, including his family members. This feeling of isolation, which many terminally ill people feel, had become a self-imposed prison.

On one visit I could clearly see what was going on, but I hardly knew him, and I felt it would be presumptuous to say anything to him about it. But as I was driving home it became crystal clear to me that I was holding myself back out of fear, and I was filled with a feeling of remorse—I saw that I was living from fear rather than from the generosity of the heart. My sense of remorse became so strong that I had to pull over. It felt like an ache in the center of my chest, and as I sat there with it, experiencing what it felt like to be caught in the narrow and constricting grip of fear, there arose a strong sense of determination not to hold myself back on my next visit. This resolve, which was generated by the experience of remorse, allowed me to speak and relate to the patient in a very different way on subsequent visits, and we quickly developed a genuine bond of the heart, one that allowed both of us to get out of our self-limiting prisons of fear.

Seeing Where and How We Get Caught

When we're caught in our emotional reactions, the first step in becoming more awake, and ultimately more genuinely happy, is to recognize clearly where and how we're caught.

We may not even know that we're angry, especially if the anger is subtle, like with impatience or mild irritability. We also may not know when anxiety or depression is on board—we may just vaguely feel that something is off. That's why asking the question "Am I truly happy right now?" followed by the question "What blocks happiness?" can be so helpful. These questions allow us to direct our attention inward and recognize, fairly specifically, what is actually going on.

Acknowledging where we're caught is a necessary first step. But it is not enough just to know that we're angry or anxious. We have to be more precise in our observations, particularly about what we're believing—we have to become aware of the stories we tell ourselves. One way to be more clear and precise is to label the thoughts that seem to carry the biggest emotional load—thoughts such as "I can't stand this" or "No one should have to put up with this." Labeling involves silently saying to ourselves, "Believing the thought *I can't stand this*." In naming the beliefs, we are not only clearly articulating them, but also diminishing some of our identification with them. In objectifying them in this way, we no longer believe them, as the solid truth. As well, the beliefs don't continue to fuel the emotions that keep us feeling separate from others.

It may be helpful to keep a notebook where you write down your most believed thoughts. It's very likely you will find the same ones recurring regularly, even in very different situations. For example, in depression, it is common to keep repeating versions of the three classic thoughts associated with feeling depressed: "My world is grim," "My life is hopeless," and "I'm no good." With almost every disconnecting emotion we entertain thoughts like, "Something is wrong here!" or "I have to fix this." And, depending on our own particular history, we get caught believing: "I'm not good enough," "I need to take control of things," "Life isn't safe," "I'll always be alone," or some other version of what we're conditioned to believe.

We also tend to solidify our emotional reactions by justifying them, based on our memories of what we've been through before. It's very seductive to look into our past and find people and events to blame for our plight. But our memories about the past are fragmented and often inaccurate. Though we may like the feeling of control that comes with analyzing the past, this is nonetheless counterproductive in that it solidifies our personal story, rather than freeing us of it.

Can we refrain from our fascination with explaining *why* we are the way we are and instead just focus on *what* we're believing in the present? No, often we cannot—because we see these beliefs as the truth, and consequently, they continue to solidify and feed our emotions. Likewise, our believed judgments also keep us caught. For example, with depression, the judgment "depression is bad" or "I shouldn't be depressed" can be more pernicious than the depression itself. So it's helpful first to recognize the specific believed thoughts and judgments that are present in the mind and then try to refrain from spinning them, so they no longer feed the emotion.

After recognizing the beliefs and refraining from them, what's next? What's next is simply what is—the physical experience of the emotion itself. Staying present with the energy and visceral texture of an emotion may seem difficult, because it will no doubt be physically uncomfortable. But there are techniques that can make this process quite straightforward.

We'll discuss the tools for doing this in the next part of the book, but one basic tool we'll return to again and again is learning how to stay with the breath into the center of the chest—the area of the body that is the seat of our emotional life. It's not that we actually breathe into the center of the chest, but as we feel the sensations of the breath as we inhale, we bring attention to the center of the chest—the area of the heart—*as if* we were breathing into it.

Many spiritual traditions make use of the heart center, just like the martial arts make use of the area below the belly button to cultivate strength. However, breathing into the chest center is not intended to cultivate strength—it is intended to cultivate awareness, openness, and receptivity. As we learn how to follow the breath into the area of the heart, in spite of whatever skepticism we may have about it, we will learn that it is a very effective tool for helping us to stay with and ultimately experience the transformation of our emotions, from something solid and dark to something much more porous and light.

We'll come back to this tool of breathing into the chest center a little later, but in the meantime, remember that we get good at what we practice. For example, in spite of our belief that we want to be happy, what percentage of our day do we practice indulging the very emotions that make us most unhappy? If we're honest, we'll see that what we've gotten good at is indulging our emotions. Instead, we must begin to practice recognizing where and how we're caught, and then practice refraining from the beliefs that feed the emotions.

Also remind yourself, with gentleness and compassion, that this is not easy, that emotional difficulties often present themselves in ways that can seem overwhelming or insurmountable. There may be times we are only capable of opening to these difficulties in small doses. Yet each moment that we do adds up. Each effort that we make—the more we practice—makes this process easier.

For now, every time you are able to identify one of your believed thoughts and then settle into your body awareness, it might be helpful to practice taking just one or two breaths into the center of the chest, just to begin to get a taste of the possibility of living in a new way. If you find it difficult to breathe in this way, I recommend practicing the following breathing exercise.

Breathing into the Center of the Chest

Sitting down on a meditation cushion or chair, take a few
deep breaths to bring awareness into the body.

Place three fingertips on the chest center, directly
between the breasts.

Press in slightly, feeling whatever sensitivity may be there.
At the very least you will feel the sensations of the
fingers against the sternum.

Become aware of the breath, and as you breathe in, feel
whatever sensations arise where your fingers rest on
the chest.

Imagine you are breathing *as if* the breath is entering the
body through the chest center, almost as if there were
a conduit right into the heart area.

Do this for just a minute or two, but come back to it
periodically throughout the day, until it feels natural
to "breathe into the chest center."

Eventually it will feel very refreshing and enlivening, as if
the breeze were going right through you.

4

Conditioned Behaviors

Genuine happiness is not the same as the absence of unhappiness. This is an important point. We can be gliding along through life with our good health, a decent job, and satisfactory relationships but still not even come close to experiencing the depth of equanimity and appreciation that are possible for us. When we're caught up in the complacency of our routines, living our life on autopilot, even if we're somewhat buffered from being actively unhappy, this is still the classic case of skating on thin ice. We're oblivious to what is really going on; all it takes is one crack in the ice—a serious threat to our health, a lost job, a relationship failure, or even something as small as being criticized or cut off on the freeway—to show us how fragile our personal "happiness" really is. We can then see how it's just a false sense of stability, based on favorable, yet temporary, external circumstances.

Even if things seem fine on the surface when we follow our usual behaviors, there may still be a deep well of unaddressed dissatisfaction. For instance, people surveyed in certain countries indicate that on the whole they are happy, yet at the same time, these countries have high suicide rates. The point is, it's possible to believe we are happy, and believe we know what makes us happy, and then pursue behaviors based on that. But the truth is, we *don't* know, and we are likely to follow strategies of behavior that bring us just the opposite.

We may believe, for example, that being in control will bring us stability and happiness, or that being liked or financially successful will make us happy. But when we pursue these strategies it's like skating on the thin ice, gliding along believing that our temporary taste of personal happiness will last indefinitely. Sooner or later, however, the anxious quiver in our being will come to the surface, and we may feel the ache of the emptiness of our pursuits, or the nagging sense that something is missing. We may then realize that something is substantially wrong. Yet, until we recognize exactly how our present way of living blocks us from the deeper experience of happiness, we will not be motivated to live any differently.

As the previous chapter pointed out, the real question we need to ask ourselves is: Why do we continue to follow behaviors that don't bring us real happiness? The answer lies in the basic human condition: that is, we are born with the innate craving for safety, security, and control—this is an integral part of our survival mechanism. We are also born with an aversion to discomfort and a natural desire for comfort and pleasure. Given these basic human predispositions, it makes sense that our learned strategies of behavior are geared to ensure that our cravings and desires are met.

On the surface, there's nothing wrong with trying to be safe or comfortable. The problem begins when our survival mode takes over and becomes our main motivation. When that happens, our other natural urges—curiosity, appreciation, and living from our true openhearted nature—are pushed aside, and consequently, our lives become narrower and increasingly less satisfying. Paradoxically, we continue to believe that our survival-based control strategies will make us happy, so we keep on trying harder or seeking approval; yet these very behaviors often bring us the most dissatisfaction.

Trying Harder

The control strategy of trying ever harder to achieve security and success makes sense on the surface. After all, making greater efforts will certainly help us achieve results—getting good grades, making more money, meeting difficult goals. And these results can, in fact, bring us a degree of personal happiness. We may feel more materially secure and even somewhat fulfilled. But this is only part of the picture. External conditions can change quickly and sometimes dramatically, such as with economic recessions or the onset of disabling medical conditions. Sometimes, as hard as we try, our efforts can't sustain our personal good fortune.

However, even if external conditions continue to be stable, there is still a price to be paid for relying on the control strategy of trying harder to bring ourselves happiness, because along with the natural desire for security, the drive to get ahead is also rooted in a fear-based need to prove ourselves. We believe that if we excel, it will demonstrate our value. Being productive becomes a means to avoid one of our most basic fears—the fear of being without worth. We may not be fully aware of this nagging inner compulsion to prove our worth, because it can be well hidden by strategies like making ourselves indispensable or staying perpetually busy. But as long as we are being driven by this fear, how can we expect to experience genuine happiness?

Throughout my youth and well into my middle years, I was driven by the need to measure up, to prove my own worth. And in a way, the strategy of trying harder served me well in that it allowed me to achieve success. Nevertheless, I was missing the fact that what little measure of happiness my efforts to excel brought me came at a cost: I was controlled by the fear underlying those efforts. If we don't recognize and address this fear, no matter how much success we achieve, the toxic fear of being without worth will keep driving us.

At some point I was fortunate enough to be able to see how this fear compelled me to continually strain and try harder, and I was able to get off the treadmill. For others, this fear is so strong, and so blind, that it drives them throughout their lives. The point is, it's easy to be seduced by the success that our efforts bring us and to equate this with happiness. But it's sad that we can be so easily deceived into calling this happiness, when at the same time the fears that drive us narrow our world and diminish the quality of our lives.

Seeking Approval

Trying harder is one very common strategy that we use in the hope that it will make us happy. Another is to seek happiness through getting approval, appreciation, or admiration. As with trying harder, which is originally based on an instinct for survival, the strategy of seeking approval is based on the survival mode of fitting into the herd. There is nothing wrong with being part of a group; however, from an early age we distort this strategy into a means of avoiding our inner pain. For example, if we have the belief that we're unworthy, or that we're nothing, we'll seek approval from others as a way to avoid having to feel our pain.

In a TV commercial I saw recently, a balding man is touting the value of surgical implants to get his hair to grow: "The most important thing in life is having fun and feeling good. And 90 percent of feeling good is *looking* good," he says. This almost sounds like a joke, but not only was he saying this seriously, the sad fact is that a lot of our behavior is based on the same assumption—that looking good will get us the approval we crave, and that this will make us happy.

As with trying harder, seeking approval may give us periods of personal happiness—after all, it feels good to be liked and appreciated. But the need for approval, as a means of avoiding our inner fears and pain, is endless, and ultimately blocks the possibility of genuine equanimity. As long as we are content with our small measure of personal happiness, whether from occasional success, approval, or some other external factor, we're unlikely to be open to exploring our human capacity for a more fundamental happiness.

Opening our eyes to what we're doing is not always easy. Our habits of behavior, like trying harder and seeking approval, can become so deeply conditioned that we can hardly see them. Even when our behaviors don't make us happy, we often don't notice because we so firmly believe that they will! One very effective way to cut through our usual blindness is to ask the following two questions: "Am I truly happy right now?" and "What blocks happiness?" To reflect on these two questions only takes a few moments, and if you do it several times a day, over a period of time you will begin to observe, very specifically, all the behaviors that directly block genuine happiness.

Addictions

Trying harder and seeking approval are two of the most widespread conditioned behaviors for achieving happiness. Almost equally common are our many addictive behaviors, starting with our addictions to pleasure and diversions. In themselves, pleasure and diversions are fine, and they can certainly make us feel good. But whenever we have addictive behaviors—whether to food, alcohol, sex, or working out—we are driven by the compulsion to keep returning to whatever we're addicted to, in the promise that it will continue to make us feel good. Ultimately, however, addictions only deliver dissatisfaction and unhappiness. Why? Because we use them to cover over our own inner unease, and the relief we get from satisfying our addictive craving is always temporary. We may feel good for a time, but because we haven't addressed that hole of neediness inside, we will feel the compulsion to cover it over with pleasure or greed or diversions again and again.

Pursuing our addictive behaviors highlights the very essence of the human tendency to misunderstand happiness. We follow these seductive behaviors because they seem to promise us happiness. And to some degree, they fulfill their promise, in that we feel happy when we experience sensual pleasure or the hit of endorphins. But the fulfillment of that promise is always temporary, and it is always based on a temporarily benevolent external environment. As long as the environment doesn't turn against us, we think our life is okay, and we don't do anything to change the situation. Nor do we address the underlying unease out of which the addictive behaviors arise: why upset the applecart when things seem to be okay? Thus, we remain on the treadmill of personal happiness/unhappiness. When we don't feel so good, we find a fix, and then we think we are happy again. The cycle goes on and on; meanwhile, genuine happiness eludes us.

Another pervasive, conditioned, addictive behavior is the need to maintain our self-image. We do whatever it takes to make sure we look a certain way, which is another form of approval seeking but with its own flavor. We all assume a self-image—the way we see and project ourselves—and the subtle belief is that this self-image or identity will make us happy. For example, an executive may have a particular self-image, reinforced by how he or she dresses, speaks, and even walks. An athlete might have a totally different self-image, often based on appearance or physical performance. Even spiritual practitioners can have a particular identity that they cherish. No matter what the self-image, the constant effort that's required to fulfill and maintain it not only drains our energy but is also the source of much of our anxiety—anxiety over the failure to live up to our ideals of how we think we're supposed to be. Without our self-image we feel exposed, both to ourselves and to others; we feel that if the truth about us were really known we would be seen as worthless or as not enough in some way.

There is perhaps no better example of how we base our happiness on a foundation of sand than the way we hold onto our self-images. We can cling to the identity of being hard-working and busy, or whatever image gives us comfort, but what happens when we lose our job and no longer feel productive, or when our knee goes bad and we can no longer do athletics, or when our mate leaves us and we feel alone and disconnected?

As with all of our conditioned behaviors, it is first necessary to see clearly what identities we cling to most. The problem is, we often get caught in our identities without knowing specifically what they are. I heard a joke recently about a cowboy who is sitting on a park bench when a woman comes and sits down next to him. She looks at his hat and boots and says, "Are you a real cowboy?" He answers, "Well, I've worked on ranches tending cows and horses all my life, so, yep, I guess I'm a real cowboy." She thinks for a moment and then says, "I'm a lesbian. I think about women when I wake up. I think about them all day long. And I think about them when I'm going to sleep." After they talk a little more she gets up and leaves. Some time later a man comes along and sits down next to him on the bench, checks him out, and asks, "Are you really a cowboy?" "Well," he answers, "I used to think I was, but now I think I'm a lesbian."

We can get very attached to our most cherished self-image; in fact, all of our conditioned behaviors are driven by our attachments and aversions. An attachment is a feeling of being emotionally bound to someone or something, which includes the *belief* that without that someone or something we cannot be happy. We can have attachment to success, security, control, or approval, as well as to our self-image.

Aversion is the negative side of attachment; we may have aversion to failure, loss, instability, or discomfort; and we usually believe that if the things toward which we feel aversion happen, we'll surely be unhappy. It can't be emphasized enough that to experience genuine happiness we first have to recognize what blocks it. This includes seeing our attachments, the things we believe will bring us happiness, but which actually do just the opposite.

We will continue to pursue the conditioned strategies of behavior that we hope will bring us happiness as long as we believe they are working. And because they sometimes do bring us some degree of personal happiness, these behaviors can get reinforced for a long time. That's how people get caught on the treadmill of their attachments and routines for a lifetime without making any effort to change. Paradoxically, we're actually fortunate if life occasionally serves us a big dose of disappointment, because it forces us to question whether our attachments and strategies really serve us. When we truly see that what we've been doing simply isn't effective in bringing us genuine happiness, we may be motivated enough to take the next step.

When I was in my late forties, I was struck with an immune system disease that left me totally disabled for many months at a time over a three-year period. I not only lost my physical vitality, which I had been very attached to, but I also felt completely marginalized—I could no longer participate in my work or in the Zen community where I had been very involved. I lost my identity as a Zen student, since I was unable to sit cross-legged or even concentrate. The activities I could do with my wife and children became limited, and so even my identities as a husband and father were undermined. A feeling of groundlessness became my pervasive reality.

Although I had been meditating for twenty years, the jolt of physical disability threw me for a proverbial loop, and for the first several weeks I couldn't make sense of things. But because the jolt was so severe, it eventually forced me to re-evaluate what I was doing with my life. For example, I began to look differently at some behaviors that I had believed without question to be worthwhile, such as the strategy of trying harder. I also began to question my meditation practice, which had been firmly rooted in the "just do it" mindset. Gradually, my approach to meditation moved to the much softer stance of "let it be." These and many other changes came directly out of the shock to my little protected world; and although in the beginning it seemed terrible, eventually I realized that being forced to reevaluate what my life was about was perhaps the single most important catalyst in coming to know the roots of genuine happiness. If I hadn't been pushed, I might never have moved beyond the complacency of the familiar.

Each of us has to examine where and how we get in our own way, observing all the ways we block fundamental happiness. We can start with seeing our sense of entitlement that life should go the way we want and expect it to go, especially the entitled beliefs that we should always be healthy and comfortable and that life should please us. We can also observe the thinking mind: with all of its laments about the past and worries about the future, with all of its blaming thoughts and the judging thoughts, including those directed toward ourselves.

We don't need to try to stop the thoughts and the entitled beliefs—for now, we just need to know, fairly specifically, what they are. The same is true with our emotional reactions; we need to observe where we get caught in our emotions, and we need to experience within ourselves how these emotions disconnect us from ourselves and others, and thus block any chance for real happiness. And finally, we need to look at all of our conditioned behaviors—our strategies of control and our addictive tendencies, including our attachments to our most cherished self-images. We've spent our whole life believing these things would give us happiness, when in fact if we look deeply, they've done just the opposite. But until we see this clearly—until we've seen the many things we do to get in our own way—we won't be motivated to go beyond our small measures of personal happiness, toward cultivating the roots of true contentment.

Part Two

The Roots of Happiness
SURRENDERING TO WHAT IS

5
Being Present

Up to this point the primary emphasis in this book has been on what blocks genuine happiness—namely, our sense of entitlement, our expectations, our believed thoughts and judgments, our fear-based emotions, and our attachments and addictions. These are the exact things that prevent us from experiencing the deeper and more lasting state of equanimity. This may sound pretty grim for a book on happiness; it may also be hard to accept that few of the things that we do to make ourselves happy actually work. But if we honestly observe ourselves, we will see that this is true. All the things we chase after in the mistaken belief that they will make us happy only give us brief periods of pleasure, at best. Externals can't make us truly happy; but genuine happiness is our natural state when all of the things that impede happiness—such as our expectations, judgments, attachments, and fears—no longer get in the way.

Additionally, there are specific roots of genuine happiness that can be directly cultivated. These roots include the innate human capacity for being present, generosity of spirit, gratitude, loving-kindness, and forgiveness. As these capacities are nourished, we become increasingly connected to our true nature, and happiness is a natural by-product. Our approach has to be twofold: we work with what gets in the way of happiness *and* we cultivate its natural roots.

Being present is one of the essential roots of true contentment. The present moment is emphasized in almost every spiritual tradition; it is talked and written about extensively; phrases like "live in the moment" and "be here now" have become common parlance. But why do we want to experience our life in the present moment? How does being present to life-as-it-is relate to the experience of genuine happiness, especially if what is happening isn't to our liking? One clear answer to that question is this: being present allows us to shift from the narrow, self-centered world of I-as-a-Me to an open and increasingly awake sense of who we truly are. As we bring attention to whatever arises in the present moment—our pretenses, our protections, our deeply held beliefs, our fears—we slowly begin to see through the seeming solidity of these self-imposed boundaries, boundaries that prevent us from seeing, and living from, what is real in each moment.

When we bring awareness to our many layers of conditioning, and to the struggles that arise out of our conditioning, the power of that conditioning is slowly diminished. This is how we can begin to experience and live not so much from the Me, but more from our natural Being. As we increasingly connect with a vaster sense of what life is, we may even have moments where we're acutely aware that we *are* the vastness, as well as a unique manifestation of it. This is where the words *connectedness* and *love* become more than just words, and it is where genuine happiness comes forth naturally. Being truly present allows us to appreciate the sweetness of the moment even when the moment isn't conventionally sweet, because, at least momentarily, we're not under the sway of the heaviness of our beliefs. The results are a lightness of being, and a sense of inner freedom.

Even when we intellectually understand the value of being present, there's still the question: What exactly does it mean to experience the present moment? It's difficult to answer this question—words can't capture the texture of being present, because the experience is not verbal or mental. Another difficulty is that being present is not just one thing—it changes from moment to moment. So instead of trying to describe it as a fixed entity, it needs to be seen and understood as more of a continuum.

What Is This Moment?

One way to enter the continuum of the present moment is by regularly asking yourself the question "What is this moment?" This is a classic Zen question, because it can't be answered by the intellect or by facts. In other words, the only way to answer it is to bypass our customary tendency of trying to understand things with the mind. So how do we answer without using the mind in the usual way? We do this by bringing attention to the physical reality of our experience.

Try this practice now. Ask yourself, "What is this moment?" To answer, first bring awareness to a very narrow band of the present moment, namely, the experience of the breath. Taking a couple of deeper breaths, specifically focus on the area in the center of the chest—feeling the texture and the changing sensations of each inhalation and exhalation. When thoughts arise, refrain from engaging them. Instead, stay with the focused experience of breathing into the chest center for the duration of a few breaths, occasionally repeating the question "What is this moment?" silently to yourself.

The focused experience of the breath is one answer to the question "What is this moment?" but it is only one narrow band of the reality of the present moment. Being mindful of one small part of our experience is a good start, but it still shuts much of life out. Now ask the question again, and this time let awareness expand to include the environment. While still feeling the breath in the center of the chest, also let awareness extend to include the room, the air, the sounds around you. You might be amazed how much enters your awareness that you would not have noticed before. Stay with the physical experience of whatever arises—actually *feeling* the air and *hearing* the sounds. When thoughts arise, you can notice them, but try not to actively engage them. Instead, bring awareness to their physical nature. For example, if you are thinking about something you need to do, simply allow the thought to pass through you, without latching onto or following it. Instead, notice *in your body* what remains. Are emotions stirred by your thoughts? If so, just acknowledge their presence. Don't ask *why*, simply *what*—perhaps there is a flutter in your belly or a knot in your throat. I will discuss working with more intense emotions later on; for now, simply stay with the purely *physical experience* of the present moment.

Continue expanding your field of awareness from the narrow focus of the breath, which is just one small part of the present moment, to include your surroundings. Then again ask the question "What is this moment?" Let awareness expand one more time, this time including not only the breath and the environment but also a more expansive or inclusive experience of what this moment actually is—the whole or gestalt physicality of simply sitting in a room, essentially doing nothing. What is the internal feeling of being alive, of being *here*, of existing in this moment?

In asking, "What is this moment?" there is still awareness of the breath and the environment, as well as the experience of just Being. Observing and feeling—resting the mind in the physical reality of simply being here—the experience is *just this*. In a way, we can say that *just this* is the only answer to the question "What is this moment?" This is not an intellectual or factual answer—it's the nonconceptual experience of the present moment.

As you can see from this exercise, there isn't a singular answer to what it means to experience the present moment, because the answer is constantly changing. It's as if the present moment were comprised of concentric circles. The first circle is very small, just one narrow band of reality—for example, the focused experience of the breath in the center of the chest. The subsequent circle represents a broader, expanding band of reality—for example, the awareness of the environment, which still includes the inner circle of awareness of breathing into the chest center. Expanding to an even wider band of what is brings us to the outermost circle, which is the bigger awareness of just Being. This circle is not separate but rather includes the awareness of each circle inside it.

Integrating these circles of awareness renders a definite sense of presence, of aliveness—sometimes the experience is one of vivid wakefulness, of "I Am Here." This is not the little "I" of the ego; it is the larger sense of who we are. Being present essentially means we're no longer caught in the head, in all of our self-centered thoughts, judgments, and expectations. We no longer identify with our thoughts or our feelings as who we are, but rather we identify with a vaster sense of what life is. Regardless of what we might be feeling physically or emotionally, we understand that we are not limited or defined by those feelings. This is the state of true contentment.

Perhaps the experience of asking "What is this moment?" was a neutral one for us, in that there wasn't any particular emotional content. But the question often arises: How is it possible to experience presence and equanimity when we're beset with stronger emotional experiences, such as anxiety? How is it possible to reside in the present moment of anxiety, when the experience is so viscerally uncomfortable? Admittedly, it's difficult to maintain awareness when anxiety arises, because to truly experience the present *as it is* means we have to refrain from our usual strategies: trying to get control, trying to figure things out, going numb, seeking diversions, or some other escape. The sole purpose of these strategies is to protect us from feeling the discomfort that we don't want to feel. But until we can refrain from these defenses, and reside in the physical experience directly, we will stay stuck in the narrow world of "me and my anxiety."

But when we ask ourselves, "What is this moment?" we are led directly into the physical experience of anxiety itself. Remember, we're not asking what the anxiety is *about*, which is analyzing—the opposite of being physically present. We're asking what it actually *is*. So we start by becoming grounded in the breath, feeling the experience of the breath in and out of the center of the chest. We stay there as long as necessary to become settled in the present-moment experience of breathing. We then let awareness expand to include the particular physical sensations in the body, such as the tightness in the chest and belly, the tension around the mouth, the overall sense of shutting down. We feel these sensations in a very focused way. Then, after a while, we include the wider circle of the environment—the air, the sounds, the sense of space in the room. We can also briefly notice and label any thoughts that come along.

Then, after we've established the awareness of the breath, the body sensations, and the environment—and this may take a while to do—we tap into the even wider circle that is the sense of our own presence. It certainly may be difficult at first to tap into this more spacious experience of the present moment, especially if we're in the midst of a strong emotional experience. However, it's at this point that we're no longer identified with the anxiety as who we are; rather, we are simply experiencing anxiety, but we are identified with awareness itself.

I don't mean to make this sound too complicated, nor do I want to make it sound too easy. The fact is, when we have discomfort like anxiety, it's counterintuitive to bring awareness to the present moment because we naturally want to turn away from, rather than toward, any form of discomfort. And once we turn toward the present moment, trying to reside in it, there will always be resistance. We may encounter resistance even when the present moment is pleasant, because the small mind of the ego—the mind of thoughts—doesn't like stepping aside, and it will forcefully attempt to reassert itself. So what is the countermeasure? It is to return again and again to the physical reality of the moment. In the next chapter we will go over numerous examples of how, specifically, to do this.

Common Detours from the Present

When you make the effort to reside in the present, there is one fact that you will undeniably encounter—*staying* present is very difficult; and we will predictably find numerous ways to detour away from the present moment. For example, one way is to jump from physically experiencing the present moment to thinking about it, mentally commenting on it, or analyzing it. That's why there is so much emphasis on returning over and over again to the physical experience, to help us avoid the detour of getting caught in the thinking mind.

A more subtle version of resistance to the present moment is when we start out with the observer mind, objectively noticing our patterns and thoughts, and then detour off into the judging mind—evaluating and finding fault. For example, we may observe that we're caught in mental spinning, and we very quickly move from simply observing to berating ourselves for not being more present. This often happens on such a subtle level that we don't even see it; however, after some practice we get better at seeing where we get caught, and we learn that the countermeasure is always to return to the physical experience of the present moment.

When emotional feelings are present and we try to reside in the present moment, one of the classic detours is to jump from being willing to simply feel the emotion to trying to change it or fix it. This form of resistance is quite natural, since we will do almost anything to avoid the discomfort of our emotions. It often takes a while to get used to seeing how readily we will jump into fix-it mode; and as we get more familiar with this tendency, it becomes easier to refrain from it.

There is, however, a more subtle way in which we avoid the present moment, one that is difficult to see. When we are experiencing an emotion like anger, and the practice instruction is to reside in the physical feeling of the anger while refraining from acting it out toward others, we can sometimes misuse the practice of refraining and turn it into suppression, where we push our unwanted feelings out of awareness. Suppressing emotions is never healthy; in the case of suppressed anger, we may even be polluting the body with the negativity of our anger. It's important to be aware of it if your tendency is to take this detour, so you can pay more attention to avoiding the mistake of suppressing the emotions you don't want to feel.

One other tempting detour from the present moment is to use awareness itself as an escape. When the present moment is not particularly pleasant, it's very seductive, particularly for meditators, to lose oneself in the more spacious experience of the breath and the environment. Granted, this will give us temporary relief, but until we work directly with whatever blocks genuine happiness, it will continue to elude us. When the present moment is unpleasant, we can learn to stay with it *and* be aware of the spaciousness of the bigger context of the breath and the environment. In this way the blockage loses its power, and at the same time we cultivate the essential quality of being present.

One other common detour from the present moment is losing sight of why we want to stay present in the first place. In fact, we frequently, and almost predictably, forget our original purpose. For example, I can't even count the number of times in my early years of practice when I found myself feeling anxious and immediately had the thought "I must become calm"—as if the point was to be calm. Only after years of practice did it finally sink in on a deeper level that the point is simply to be present, to willingly reside in what is, *exactly* as it is—calm or agitated, pleasant or unpleasant. Otherwise we're trying to avoid something when we don't even know what it is. We can also forget our original purpose by inadvertently using our efforts to feed the ego-mind—the mind that's always trying to get somewhere. For example, when we get caught identifying with the "I" in "*I'm* going to be present," we've added a layer of unnecessary striving to our otherwise genuine aspiration to live in a more awake way.

Here's another example of the bizarre ways our thinking becomes distorted, where we completely lose sight of the original purpose of refraining from particular activities. A devout religious couple go to their spiritual counselor with some questions about their upcoming wedding day. The man begins by saying, "We'd really like to be able to dance at our wedding reception. Is that okay?" The counselor emphatically replies, "Absolutely not! Dancing will lead you to the devil."

The woman is a little shaken, and she asks, "But what about sex? Is it okay to have sex?" "Yes," says the counselor, "the Bible says to be fruitful and multiply." She quickly responds, "Is it okay if I'm on top?" "Yes, that's fine—you can still be fruitful and multiply."

The man then asks, "Can we do it standing up?" "Definitely not!" shouts the counselor. "Why not?" the man asks. "Because that could lead to dancing!" cries the counselor.

We can laugh at our all-too-human tendency to distort things and forget our purpose, and it's certainly better to laugh than to judge and berate ourselves, but we still need to pay attention to our own version of this tendency, so it doesn't take us off course.

The one other very common detour away from the present moment comes from misunderstanding an often-repeated phase: "Just let it go." When we're experiencing an old destructive pattern or a difficult emotion, it's very common for someone to give us the well-intended advice to let it go. What this means is that we should simply drop it. After all, why should we continue to carry old baggage that harms us? But is it ever really that simple? Can we really just let something go because we see that it is unnecessary or harmful? The truth is, if life were that easy we would have let go of our obstacles to happiness already, and we'd all be genuinely happy right now. Granted, with some emotions or patterns that aren't too deeply ingrained, we can occasionally let them go. But with most difficult things, simply letting them go is not really an option.

However, there is another, more realistic, option: we can learn to let our difficult experiences *just be*. This is what it means to reside in our experiences without trying to change or get rid of them. As we breathe into the center of the chest, we can learn to reside in what is. This is the essence of letting be; it is also the equanimity of just Being. When we truly reside in what is, there is no one special to be and nothing special to do. As the breath flows in and out of the chest center, and we let life be as it is—no longer needing to let go of anything—we taste the appreciation of genuine happiness.

This may be particularly challenging given that Western culture measures worth through *doing*, through being active and productive. The concept of simply *being* holds little value and is, for most people, somewhat foreign. It may even sound passive or lazy. Yet, experiencing the present moment—*surrendering to what is*—is a portal into reality, into a more spacious experience of what life is. And every moment in which we experience ourselves within this larger context cultivates one of the essential roots of genuine happiness. Being present in this way allows us to experience the innumerable delights of existence, such as the delicious feel of a cool breeze on a warm day, or the beauty of a trail of ants zigzagging their way on the pavement, or the preciousness of the sight of someone you love sleeping peacefully in bed.

Granted, learning to surrender to the present moment is

challenging, but it's also something we can gradually learn how to do. And the more we practice staying present during the less intense or even neutral moments in life, the easier it will become to remain present during the most intense and difficult experiences. The real question is whether we're willing to give up the familiar—all the ways we've tried to find happiness that have only brought us dissatisfaction. Only when we've reached that critical understanding of what needs to be done can we willingly follow the most fundamental instruction of Zen practice: become present as often as possible and reside there as long as possible.

6

Three Questions

In order to experience the genuine happiness of equanimity we need to do two things: first, recognize and work with what blocks it; and second, learn to cultivate the natural roots of happiness. I have found a fairly simple and very effective way of combining these two aspects, through regularly asking myself three straightforward questions: Am I truly happy right now? What blocks happiness? Can I surrender to what is?

In general, I consider myself genuinely happy, including the times when my immune system disorder flares up and I have nausea and intense physical discomfort. Even during these periods, which sometimes last for days or even weeks, I am still generally cheerful, primarily because I don't get caught in the sense of entitlement—the voice that tells us life should go the way we want it to go. Nor do I allow the fearful thoughts, based in an imagined future of continuing discomfort, to get any traction. Nonetheless, there are still times when old patterns come up that block happiness.

For over a year, I've asked myself these three questions in all different situations, from the most neutral to the most intense. It's been very interesting to observe all the different ways that happiness can be impeded. It's also been quite exciting to see how the effort to be present, by directly residing in physical reality, can undercut these impediments, sometimes even immediately.

1. Am I truly happy right now?

The first question is a way to simply recognize how we're feeling in the present moment. Quite often, we're not even aware that we're unhappy: for example, our unhappiness may be subtle, as when we're mildly impatient or irritated; or sometimes, it can be entirely hidden, as when we're feeling comfortable and complacent. But being comfortable and content is not the same as genuine happiness, and it is very easy to let our life slip by unaware of what we're missing. Asking this simple question is a way of recognizing our current state, and it is the necessary wake-up to what comes next.

2. What blocks happiness?

The second question is a little more difficult to answer. It requires scanning our experience to see where we're caught—in thoughts, emotions, or behaviors. In the beginning, we may not be clear about what we're thinking or feeling, and it may take some practice in getting to know ourselves before we can begin to answer the question fairly quickly. It may be useful to keep a journal on hand to both explore and catalog your responses to this question.

Sometimes the only answer that comes to the second question is "I don't know." These are the times when we can't clearly see where or how we're caught. In this situation, we periodically return to the second question, so that we can eventually recognize, quite specifically, what is blocking happiness. Once we see clearly where we're stuck we can move on to the third question.

3. Can I surrender to what is?

The third question is not the surrender of resignation or giving in. It's about stopping our struggle to change our experience or to avoid it. It's about fully entering into our experience— residing in the physical reality of the present moment. It is similar to the question used in the last chapter, "What is this moment?" When we ask this third question, it not only addresses what blocks happiness, but it also directly cultivates the quality of being present to what is, *exactly as it is*—a quality that naturally fosters both equanimity and appreciation, two of the essential aspects of true contentment.

When asking this third question, it is very helpful to take a couple of deep breaths into the center of the chest; this takes us immediately out of the head and allows the answer to come from residing in exactly what we are experiencing. Even when the experience is uncomfortable, as it often is with sadness or anxiety, we can learn to enter into the physical reality of the experience, if only for the duration of a few breaths. The point is to leave the mental realm, where most of our unhappiness takes root and grows, and enter into the nonconceptual experience of the present moment, which is purely physical. To make this process more clear, let's look at a few examples of how asking these three questions actually works in some everyday situations.

Using the Three Questions in Daily Life

In the Car

You're driving on the freeway when traffic comes to an almost complete stop. As far as you can see in front of you, the cars are barely moving. You're already late to where you're going, and you can feel your stomach tightening at the thought of being stuck in traffic with no idea of when you'll get to your destination.

You remember the three questions, and as soon as you ask, "Am I truly happy right now?" the answer "No!" flashes across your mental screen. You then ask, "What blocks happiness?" and as you scan your experience it becomes clear that what you're feeling the most—and what is blocking any sense of happiness—is irritation and impatience.

When you ask, "Can I surrender to what is?" you start by taking a couple of deep breaths into the center of the chest to ground yourself in physical reality. Residing in the present moment, you feel the tightness throughout the body, the rigidity around the mouth, the heat behind the eyes. You also hear the soundtrack of your mind: "I hate having to wait in traffic." "This sucks!" "Why is this happening to me?" Staying with the breath and the physical experience in the body, you gradually become aware of the environment, noticing the clouds and the air temperature. With this more expansive experience of the present moment, the thoughts are no longer so compelling. You begin to see the theme of entitlement more clearly—how your emotional reaction of impatience is the direct result of the entitled belief that life owes you something or that you aren't supposed to be inconvenienced.

Surrendering to what is—not trying to replace your impatience with patience but rather just feeling its texture—allows the experience to change on its own. A wave of relaxation flows through you, and you become aware that you are no longer feeling caught in impatience. Staying with the breath and taking in the view all around you—the cars, the buildings, the clouds—you realize that you're perfectly okay sitting waiting in traffic. The phrase "nowhere to go" passes through your mind, and for the first time you truly understand what these words mean.

At Work

You're working on a project for your job, and you're having a lot of trouble completing it. You begin questioning yourself, and old feelings of self-doubt and anxiety gradually undermine your sense of competency. Your mood turns sour, and your world begins to feel narrow and dark. The feeling is a familiar one, and the mind adds the soundtrack, "After all these years, I still feel the same. Nothing will ever change." The sense that life is grim becomes pervasive, but you notice a note taped to your computer that reads: "Ask the three questions."

Upon asking, "Am I truly happy right now?" the mind immediately replies, "How could anybody be happy in this situation?" But you stay with the process nonetheless, and ask the second question, "What blocks happiness?" You are feeling so overwhelmed that it is not clear to you what is actually going on. You notice that you are upset and depressed, and you conclude that the main impediment to experiencing happiness is feeling and believing that everything is wrong.

Even though you don't have much confidence that it will help, something in you still wants to be free, and you proceed with the third question, "Can I surrender to what is?" Starting with a deep breath into the center of the chest, you immediately feel the sensation of heaviness in your chest. You experience the physical contraction in your neck and shoulders, and you feel your lips tightly pressed together. You continue to follow the breath into the chest center, and one thought seems to keep surfacing: "I'm worthless." The original feeling of sourness gradually feels more like sadness, and you try to stay with the texture of that feeling in the body, breathing it into the chest center along with the inbreath.

After a couple of minutes you feel like you can't take it anymore, so you get busy straightening up your desk, then looking out the window. The blue sky reminds you of the instructions for staying present, and you immediately go back to the breath and the feelings in the body. As soon as you feel a little grounded, you expand awareness to include the sense of space in the room, as well as the view of the sky out your window. You make an effort to refrain from getting hooked into the repeating thoughts of worthlessness, and instead you continue to reside in the physical experience of body and environment. Within a short time the breath becomes deeper and more calming, and in a momentary insight you see how you've been caught in the self-judgmental mind—the mind that tells you that you'll never measure up. But on clearly seeing this self-judgment for what it is—*just a thought!*—it loses its power. Although the thought remains, you no longer believe it in the same way, and the heaviness and grimness rapidly dissipate. You ask yourself again if you are now happy, and although hesitant to say yes, you nonetheless find yourself feeling genuine equanimity.

In Relationship

You're in a personal relationship that has had its share of ups and downs. One day, during a disagreement, some things are said that make you feel like you've been punched in the stomach. You believe the criticism to be unjustified, and you vigorously defend yourself. But pretty quickly the anger takes over, and you feel like you're ready to explode. Fortunately, you agree to a truce, but when you retreat to solitude, you find you're still seething with anger.

You remember the three questions, including the instruction not to skip the first question—"Am I truly happy right now?"—even when the answer seems obvious. When you ask it, you're surprised to find that it hadn't yet occurred to you that you were feeling unhappy. The anger is so strong it has taken over completely, leaving little room for awareness of anything else.

When asking the second question—"What blocks happiness?"—the first thing that comes to mind is that you're feeling very angry. You're not sure you want to go on to the third question—"Can I surrender to what is?"—because you can't imagine any positive outcome. But in asking the second question, you glimpse that your hesitancy to go to the third question stems from the fact that you *want* to stay angry, to be right—and you notice that you don't really want to give it up, even when it's obviously blocking genuine happiness. This is a startling realization, and you let the impact of this settle in before you begin to work with the third question.

Following the instructions for residing in what is, you start with a few deeper breaths into the center of the chest. Then you focus on the specific bodily sensations: the feeling of heat and tightness, the explosive energy coursing through the body, the clenched fists and pursed lips. It's difficult to stay with these feelings in the body, because the strong thoughts of blame and self-righteousness keep taking hold. You can feel the seductive sense of juiciness and power when you get caught in "being right," so you make a stronger effort to refrain from indulging the thoughts. With a firm sense of resolve, you turn away from indulging the thoughts of blame every time they arise, and instead you reside in the physical experience in the body, simply noticing and experiencing what is there—not *why*, just *what*.

As the explosive energy of anger begins to quiet down, you drop down a layer and realize you are now experiencing the more vulnerable feelings of hurt and sadness. The thoughts are no longer as strong, but they still threaten to highjack your attention. Each time they begin, you refrain from them and return to residing in the body. After a while, you drop down another layer, where you experience the feeling of fear—particularly of being rejected and alone. You continue to breathe into the center of the chest, breathing the physical sensations of fear into the heart with the inbreath.

You remember to include the environment, becoming aware of the sounds coming in from the outside and of the quality of light in the room. Staying with this bigger container of awareness, the experience of fear begins to diminish. Although it still remains, you are no longer invested in being right, and you become aware that the person who criticized you is probably hurting just as much as you are. As your body softens, you feel compassion for yourself as well as for the other person.

Then, taking another breath into the center of the chest, something opens up, and you feel vividly aware. Remnants of anger and fear remain, but it is clear to you that these emotions are not you. The energy of anger and fear has transformed, and you experience a much vaster sense of what life is.

When You've Got Nothing to Do

You're feeling sort of content; at least nothing seems wrong. The only trouble is that you have two free hours with nothing to do. You're used to being very busy, and pretty soon you begin feeling a very uncomfortable vacuum inside. The mind anxiously asks, "What next?" You go to the computer and start playing online games, and after a short while you're totally hooked. There's a vague knowing in the back of your mind that you're wasting time—letting your life drift by as if you had endless time. But the chemicals flowing through the body, triggered by the stimulus of playing on the computer, override the brief moments of remorse.

You remember to ask the three questions. To the first question—"Am I truly happy right now?"—you quickly answer, "Yes." You are feeling stimulated by the addictive pull of the computer, and the unease you were feeling earlier—the gnawing feeling of emptiness at having nothing to do—is no longer on the surface. But you pause to look a little deeper. You wonder if what you are feeling is really happiness or whether perhaps it is just a tepid complacency brought on by your addictive attachment to computer games. You become aware that as soon as you stop playing you will no longer be buffered from the unease you were feeling earlier, and that the "happiness" you are presently feeling is really just a temporary "fix."

You change your answer to the first question to "No." And although you feel resistance to asking the second question—

"What blocks happiness?"—you ask it anyway. You immediately feel uncomfortable and adrift. You feel the strong urge to go back to the computer or to occupy yourself in some other way. However, you pause just long enough to see your hidden agenda—that is, your unconscious attempt to cover over the growing unease inside you. Once the door of clarity opens, it rapidly becomes apparent that your addictive behaviors—not just with the computer, but with business or overeating or cleaning or organizing or drinking—are what block the possibility of genuine equanimity, because they prevent us from ever fully experiencing the angst that lurks at our core. And thus, we are never completely free of it.

When you ask the third question—"Can I surrender to what is?"—you don't quite know what to do. You remember to start by taking a few breaths into the center of the chest. Then you focus on the specific physical sensations in the body—the overall feeling of antsyness, the uncomfortable feelings of tightness in the stomach and chest, the physical urge to "do" something. As you become more aware of the physical body, the mind cries out louder for relief: "What now? I need to *do* something!" But a quieter voice reminds you to just stay. You refrain from the addictive pull and stay with the physical discomfort, and it becomes increasingly obvious that this discomfort is at the root of all of your addictive behaviors.

Staying with the discomfort is difficult. The mind keeps darting off to avoid the feelings in the body, primarily by trying to analyze why you feel the way you do. But you keep returning to the breath in the center of the chest and the physical experience in the body. At some point you then remember to broaden the field of awareness by including the environment—the feeling of space in the room and the sounds of traffic from outside. Awareness shifts back and forth between the internal bodily sensations and the physical reality of the environment, and gradually the somberness of mood begins to lighten. There is a sudden realization that you don't have to struggle—that *there's nothing to do*. It becomes clear that all of the struggle, the addictive craving, the need to fill the gnawing unease with activities and substances, are compulsions that you don't have to follow. There's a sense of freedom in realizing that even though the addictive tug may be strong, you don't have to be pulled in by it. You see that by simply residing in what is, *exactly* as it is, the much more genuine experience of happiness can begin to arise naturally on its own.

Concluding Thoughts on the Three Questions

The above examples are composites of my own and others' experiences—experiences that sometimes took days to unfold. One thing to keep in mind is that there is no specific formula for how to answer the three questions. Answering them, just like living, is more an art form than a set of rules to follow. Nonetheless, there are certain general guidelines that are helpful.

The guidelines can be summed up as the three *R*s—recognizing, refraining, and residing. First, you have to *recognize* what you're doing—what you're thinking and what you're feeling. Second, you have to *refrain* from repeating the thoughts and judgments, and sometimes also from engaging in compulsive actions. Last, you need to *reside* in the physical experience of the present moment, including feeling the breath in the center of the chest, the specific sensations in the body, and finally the broader experience of the environment. Residing in, or surrendering to, the present moment is what ultimately allows transformation to take place.

Based on the premise that we get good at what we practice, you may find it helpful to devote a whole day to periodically asking the three questions, to get a feel for how to work with them. It's important to be disciplined in your efforts and to persevere throughout the day. But this doesn't mean you have to be grim. We can be serious in our purpose without being somber. It's possible instead to be gentle in our efforts, which means we're not getting caught up in all of the "shoulds" of the self-judgmental mind, such as the grim self-judgment "I *should* be more present."

If you're sincere in your aspiration to live more genuinely, there's no way to do this wrong. We will certainly take many detours from the present moment. We will want to turn away from discomfort again and again. But with every detour, with every turning away, all we have to do to get back on track is to return to one breath into the center of the chest. A wise person once said, "Anything worth doing is worth doing half-assed." Can we give up our ideals of perfection and simply lighten up and do the best we can at the moment? Asking the three questions, and attempting to answer them the only way we can in the moment, begins to open the doors to the reality of genuine happiness—a reality we may not have even imagined was possible.

7

Emotional Freedom

One of the most powerful barriers to being truly happy is being caught in divisive emotional reactions, such as anger, fear, and despair. Yet these very reactions can serve as an accelerated path to transformation, from the narrow self-centered world of Me to the equanimity of true contentment. Sooner or later in spiritual practice we will have to address the inevitable clash between what we want and what is—the clash out of which all of our separating emotional reactions, and much of our unhappiness, arise. When this clash occurs, where life does not give us what we want, the emotional reaction can be quite powerful, and it often feels very messy when we're in the midst of it. In these moments it's almost as if our ability to think clearly goes on sabbatical, and we quickly fall into old, destructive habits, such as dumping our emotions on others, judging our feelings as bad, or suppressing our experience altogether.

When we get caught in these negative patterns we are clearly disconnected from ourselves. Each time we indulge these patterns another layer of armoring is placed over the heart, and consequently the unhappiness of feeling separate increases. We can't always avoid this dark place because life will never give us everything we want; but we can learn how these experiences can become transformative. Learning how to work directly with our divisive emotional reactions is key; practice allows the dark and negative energy to be transformed—like turning poison into honey. As we become decreasingly caught in our emotions, it's increasingly possible to experience the happiness of inner freedom.

Learning to Welcome Difficult Emotions

One crucial aspect of working with our emotions is learning to stop viewing them as obstacles to our happiness. We almost always judge the emotions that *feel* bad as bad; we see them as the enemy, as something to be conquered or eradicated. At the very least we want to change them so we won't feel so uncomfortable. But from the point of view of spiritual practice, these views are actually upside down. Our negative emotions are neither obstacles to our happiness, nor are they the enemy. In fact, these very emotions, *when worked with consciously*, are our exact path to the genuine happiness of equanimity.

When we are forced to attend to the places where we are most stuck, such as when faced with our anger and fear, we have the perfect opportunity to go to the roots of our attachments. This is why we repeatedly emphasize the need to welcome such experiences, to invite them in, to see them as our path. Normally we may only feel welcoming toward our pleasant experiences, but Buddhist practice asks us to welcome *whatever* comes up, including the unpleasant and the unwanted, because we understand that only by facing these experiences directly can we become free of their domination. In this way, they no longer dictate who we are.

What I find most helpful is to "say yes" to my experience. Saying "yes" doesn't mean that I like my experience; it's a way of becoming curious about what it is, and being willing to *feel* it. It also means I'm willing to see my experience from a different point of view: instead of seeing it as an obstacle, I see it as a direct path to freedom. For example, saying "yes" to fear means inviting it in, in order to feel it as the present-moment experience of our life. We don't think about it or analyze it or do anything with it; we simply surrender to what is there. How different is this from what we normally do, which is to push it away? Saying "yes" to our emotions, by welcoming them in, allows us to move from seeing our emotions as the enemy to actually befriending them. This in itself lightens us up considerably. When anger or fear arises, instead of thinking, "Oh no, not this!" we can remember to say, "Yes! Here it is again—what will it feel like this time?" As we raise the mind of curiosity, gloominess and dread are replaced with the natural excitement of exploration and discovery.

Learning to see our negative emotions as a spiritual path does not come easily, especially when deep conditioning arises. We often remain stuck in old patterns of response, but even these deeply seated patterns can lose their power over us. As an example, I live fairly close to the Pacific Ocean, and I love to go boogie boarding whenever I'm having a period of good health. But even though I love it, I still have to deal with old fear-based conditioning every time I go in the water. I grew up in Atlantic City and spent nearly every summer day in the ocean. Twice I almost drowned and had to be saved by the lifeguards, and the panic I felt in those moments made a deep visceral impact. As a young boy I also witnessed several hurricanes, and during one of them, I watched the incredible force of the ocean literally rip up the wooden boardwalk. From that time on, the deeply conditioned memory of fear and powerlessness has automatically been triggered whenever I go to the ocean.

When I'm about to go out on my boogie board, especially when the waves are big, my stomach instinctively tightens as my mind wordlessly flashes "Danger!" If I listened to my mind, I would never go in. Or, I might try to "Be strong," by running into the water, hoping to overcome and get rid of my fears. But this would not be real strength, nor would it truly address the fear. So when that uncomfortable feeling of danger arises, I've learned to say "yes" to it. This is not the same as trying to be strong and overcome it. Saying "yes" simply means being willing to welcome the fear in, to be curious about how it feels, and to surrender to it, just as it is. It also means I'm willing to see the fear as my path to freedom—not by trying to get rid of it, but by no longer letting it dictate who I am or what I do. As I befriend the fear, I can actually relate to it as just the conditioning that it is. This is the essence of the practice of loving-kindness—being able to relate to our emotions with a friendliness that no longer sees them as defects or proof that there is something wrong with us; instead, we learn to relate to them with a benign tolerance for simply being human. So when I go into the water and ride the waves in, even if some of the stomach tightness remains, the overall experience is not only free of the dark constriction of fear, it is often wonderfully light and joyous.

Learning to welcome our difficult emotions, and to understand how they are actually the path to inner freedom, is crucial in working with our separating emotional reactions. It is also important, as we attempt to reside directly in them, to check out any strong thoughts we might be believing in the moment. Whenever we're caught in an emotional reaction, we can be certain that there are beliefs on board that we're not seeing quite clearly. These beliefs tend to feed the emotion and guarantee that we will remain stuck. So to clarify our beliefs, we can ask, "How is it supposed to be?"—which will point to our hidden expectations. Or we can ask, "What is the most believed thought?" Even if we don't get to the most believed thought, chances are we will at least be able to see and label some of the thoughts we may not have been aware of before. These are the thoughts that would normally block any effort to truly reside in and feel the emotion. Thoughts like, "This isn't fair" and "What's going to happen to me?"

may not sound like much, but their power to solidify our emotional reactions should not be underestimated.

At a recent retreat where I was teaching, I woke up on the last morning feeling very dark. Nothing had happened to trigger the somber mood, but it was nonetheless very strong. Classic thoughts of doom began running through my mind: "Life is bleak," "Everything is hopeless," and so forth— and they were incredibly compelling. I asked myself the three questions, and to the second question—What blocks happiness?—it was clear that being caught in these believed thoughts not only blocked happiness, but also prevented me from residing in the present-moment experience. However, as strong as the thoughts were, I was also very aware that the thoughts were not the truth. And seeing this clearly, that they were *just thoughts*, allowed me to step outside of them. They still remained, but as I addressed the third question—Can I surrender to what is?—it became possible to simply watch the thoughts with interest. What was most interesting was how compelling the thoughts were; and it reminded me that having a spiritual practice doesn't mean that these dark clouds won't go through us, or that they won't sometimes grip us. It also became clear that it was possible to experience equanimity even while the thoughts remained, so long as I refrained from giving credence to them. By not fighting them or judging them, but just seeing them clearly, they lost their power.

Over the years, as we observe our emotional highs and lows, we will come to one inescapable conclusion: the way we view ourselves—as a solid, permanent self—is one of our most deeply seated illusions. A more realistic view is that we are a complex collection of many "Me's." In one moment we may believe strongly that life is too hard and that we can't cope. Then, ten minutes later we can feel that everything is fine. Or, we wake up feeling anxious or grouchy, and this Me totally colors our perception of reality. But sooner or later that Me will be replaced by another Me, that may seem equally real and true. Once we understand that our emotional life is strongly determined by whichever Me is presenting itself, we can learn to take a step back.

One of my favorite practices is called "It does." Whenever I catch myself believing in one of my many Me's, such as when I hear myself thinking or saying, "I'm irritated" or "I'm feeling crummy," I change the words to "*It's* irritated" or "*It's* crummy." This simple change in language, which is a form of labeling, immediately makes the perspective more spacious, and I no longer feel so invested in that particular Me as the truth. Understanding that we are composed of many Me's, and labeling each Me as "It," fosters a sense of lightheartedness and a taste of emotional freedom.

This is an example of how watching and labeling our thoughts allows us to stop identifying with them, and to recognize that they're not the objective truth. However, there are times when our thoughts are unrelenting, and just watching them may not be enough. When emotion-based thoughts are this powerful, a different kind of effort might be required. In these cases, it may be necessary to forget about gentle observation for a while and instead use the sword. Every single time the obsessive thoughts arise you say, "Cut!"—and then return to feeling the energy of the emotion coursing through the body. Even if you have to do it a hundred times, keep cutting the thoughts until the addictive cycle is broken. At that point you can go back to simply watching, because the thoughts will no longer be overpowering. I don't recommend using this approach unless it's absolutely necessary, but it's good to keep it in mind, because at times it may be the only thing that works.

It should be obvious that working with our negative emotional reactions is often messy, and rarely straightforward. Sometimes the inner feelings are quite chaotic, and there may be no clear view of what to do. This is where asking the three questions can be so helpful, because they can guide us directly where we need to go, step by step. Asking the first question—"Am I truly happy right now?"—may seem unnecessary, but we might be surprised how often we're not aware of what we're feeling. The second question—"What blocks happiness?"—is also crucial, because unless we can clearly see where we're stuck, how can we expect to address it effectively? The third question—"Can I surrender to what is?"—goes to the heart of the transformative process. As we begin to answer this question, it's helpful to first remember to welcome our difficult emotion as our spiritual path. Then we remember to clearly see our believed thoughts. At this point residing in the physical experience of the present moment, which is admittedly difficult, can be much more straightforward.

In Our Darkest Moments

Sometimes, however, our emotions can feel so overwhelming that no matter what we do we remain entrenched in them. When we experience these dark moments, even asking the three questions may not help. These are the moments, whether of sadness, fear, or despair, when we feel most disconnected from the heart. These are also the times when we often judge ourselves most harshly, where we firmly believe that we're a failure. Yet, even in these darkest moments, there is still one thing that we can do—we can take one single breath into the center of the chest. And with that, perhaps we can notice one thought; or feel just one sensation; or become aware of the environment. And then we can take just one more breath into the chest center. Using the breath as a conduit, we can breathe the sensations of distress and discouragement right into the heart. Each single breath into the center of the chest helps us open to what we're feeling, and slowly the sense of disheartenment can dissolve into reconnection.

In our darkest moments, where there is so little compassion for ourselves, breathing into the heart is in itself an act of compassion. The very process of opening to our deep well of personal pain, opens us to the universal pain of being human. Breathing the emotion into the center of the chest undermines the seductive power of the emotion-based thoughts, and we no longer feel so trapped and alone. Even when the distress remains, we can get a taste of the healing power of the spaciousness of the heart, and this allows us to eventually come back to the basic practice of being present.

When I was in my early fifties, I went through a three-year period where I would wake up between three and five o'clock in the morning, usually with unending anxiety. My mind would jump from one thing to another—my work, my health, my relationships—and wherever my mind would land there was anxiety. It certainly seemed that the content of my anxiety was what was causing me to wake up, but after a while it became clear that the things my mind would spin around were not the cause—they simply added fuel to the fire. At one point I made up a blanket thought, one that labeled all the varied contents: "Having a believed thought things are out of control—I've got to get control." I silently repeated this thought label as often as necessary until I was no longer caught in the mental spinning.

Although this was helpful, the physical experience of anxiety was still very strong. I tried getting up, I tried meditating, but when I'd get back in bed the anxiety was still there. Sometimes it got so strong I couldn't lie still—I occasionally felt like I wanted to jump out of my own skin. As this continued night after night, I began to get very discouraged. Not only was I tired and anxious, but my many years of meditating didn't seem to help. Nor did the various practice techniques that I had experienced with so much success in the past. At one point I started dreading waking up at night, knowing it would be like two hours of torture.

Then a strange thing happened. I was listening to a Bob Dylan song in which one of the lines was, "They say the darkest hour is right before the dawn." Even though this is something of a cliché, a light bulb went on, and I realized the truth expressed in this line. How often had I experienced this in the past—where the darkest moments would eventually open into just the opposite. I had forgotten this, and was just trying to get through the hours of darkness without seeing what a valuable opportunity they were. It was then that I started to lie on my back, no longer looking at the clock or worrying about how much sleep I would miss, and instead just followed the breath into the center of the chest. This was a fairly new practice for me at the time, but something about it drew me in. Sometimes I could only do one breath before being pulled back into the anxiety and discouragement. But after a while, as I learned how to breathe the physical sensations of anxiety right into the chest center along with the inbreath, I was able to surrender to it.

Gradually it became clear to me that the anxiety I was experiencing in the night was the basic human fear of powerlessness, of having limited time. And as I was able to reside in it for longer and longer periods, the feelings of anxiety and disheartenment gradually transformed into a deeper understanding of what my life was actually about. Now, many years later, when I occasionally wake up in the night, I don't mind lying awake. I simply breathe into the chest center and use it as a precious opportunity to dwell deeply in the heart. During these moments I feel a deep sense of connection; and the experience is one of genuine happiness.

When we are caught in the darker and more intense emotions, and our life seems most difficult, we normally believe that this difficulty prevents us from being happy. But this belief is based on the false assumption that happiness requires that our life go smoothly. We are forgetting one of the deepest truths of spiritual practice: we can't be truly happy *until* our life is difficult. Difficulties push us to the edge of where we're stuck; our darkest emotional reactions tell us that we're in the exact right place to experience emotional freedom, *if* we're willing to work with them consciously. This means being willing to say yes to our emotions and invite them in.

How this transformative process works is a mystery. Whether we're caught in anger, fear, or despair, in each case the disconnecting emotion is held together in a tightly woven complex of beliefs, protections, and physical memories, stored in the very cells of the body. This is what it means to live out of our conditioning, and we often feel that we can't do anything to impact it. Nevertheless, when the emotional experience of disconnection arises—where we feel separate from ourselves as well as from others—if we consciously reside in that exact experience of separation, we can—sometimes gradually and sometimes suddenly—see through the solidity of the emotions we're holding onto.

When we bring awareness to our beliefs and to the physical experience in the body, that tightly held sense of "self" begins to unravel. As we breathe into the chest center and feel the emotion fully, particularly when awareness of environmental air or sounds is included as well, the layers of armoring begin to dissolve, and we can reconnect with the heart, and with a vaster sense of what life is. Although the process is mysterious, it's clear that surrendering to our emotions in the present moment is nonetheless the direct transformative path to inner freedom and equanimity. When our barriers of protection finally come down, all that remains is happiness.

8

Meditation

Meditation is no longer an esoteric activity practiced primarily in monasteries; it is now commonly recognized as beneficial for all sorts of things, including reducing stress and promoting good health. For these reasons, many people are inclined to try it, and this is certainly a good thing. But using meditation to relieve stress or as an aid to good health is still in the realm of chasing after personal happiness. When we use meditation as a tool to feel better, to become calm, or to lower our blood pressure, we are basically trying to change life to suit us. But what good is it to have nice experiences during meditation if we don't also address the anger and fear that we all carry within us, which will inevitably undermine our good feelings? Enjoying periods of calm is understandable; but if we use meditation as yet another way to feel better, and at the same time expect it to bring us the deeper happiness of true contentment, we will probably be disappointed.

There are, however, many different ways to meditate that are not an attempt to bypass life's difficulties. Some forms of meditation can, in fact, not only help cultivate the roots of genuine happiness but also aid in working with what blocks it. The meditation technique described in this chapter, which is a form of Zen meditation that I've been doing for many years, is geared to serve this dual purpose. I'm also including specific instructions on how to meditate at the end of the chapter.

Sitting in meditation is one of the best ways to allow the mind and body to settle down. The intention, when sitting in stillness and silence, is to be as fully present as possible with *whatever* you are experiencing. The point is not to feel calm, although this certainly might happen as the mind and body settle. The point is to be *aware*, and to cultivate the ability to reside in what is. It's interesting that the word *reside* literally means to sit, remain, or abide.

The path of spiritual practice implores us to do the simplest yet most difficult thing: to sit still and just be present. To reflect without thinking. There is no action involved, only stillness and observation. In meditation, we let whatever comes up, come up. We invite it in. We welcome all of it, including the resistance, the boredom, the judgments, the endless mental spinning. We let it come up and then we watch it. We don't think, we don't analyze, we don't judge—we simply watch and experience.

When things come up that we don't like, we try to remember that these thoughts and feelings are our teachers, in that we can learn from them. They're not an enemy to conquer or get away from. In other words, don't try to change your experience—just be aware. Simply watch with curiosity as your experience unfolds, without trying to make yourself different. Doing this means we'll no longer have to live out of our cherished self-images—for example, being a calm, clear, or "together" person. In other words, we don't have to look "spiritual." Instead, can we just acknowledge who we are— including all of our so-called shortcomings? The question is, can we give up our ideals of perfection?

Again, the point is to watch, to reflect, without judging or analyzing. Watching all the reflections of our many Me's—all the ways we present ourselves—is one way to bring the quality of kindness to ourselves, just as we are. We no longer feel the need to make so much of an effort to present ourselves in some special way. Needing to be special keeps us solidly stuck in unhappiness. Thus, during meditation, we simply *watch* the need to be special, *notice* the self-images we're holding to, and *feel* what that is. Even if we cannot do so with genuine compassion, at the very least we need to try to do so without judgment.

Simply watching allows us to stop struggling, to stop trying so hard to prove something, to measure up—all in order to cover over whatever sense of lack we carry in our core. It certainly may feel frightening or strange when we first stop struggling, because we've grown accustomed to striving as a way of being, and we feel anxious about leaving the comfort of the familiar. But when we stop the struggle of trying to measure up, to get somewhere, we then have the space— the actual inner spaciousness—to be at home with ourselves. Learning to be at home with ourselves—and this is no easy task—is one of the prime benefits of meditation practice.

We also have to remember that meditation practice is never a straight line to a fixed goal: periods of clarity often give way to confusion; aspiration may interweave with discouragement; and moments of feeling like a failure are bound to mix with moments of going deeper. So through all of these ups and downs, the practice is simply to rest your mind in the breath, to feel it fully. Once you can experience the breath, rest your mind in the environment—feeling the air, hearing the sounds, sensing the spaciousness of the room. Then let awareness of the breath and the environment be experienced together. This dual awareness of the breath and the environment is our anchor, and we can feel the sense of presence in staying with this experience. Let whatever else arises be included within this wider awareness, including the mindless daydreams, the compulsion to plan, the urge to have internal conversations, the moments of spacing out, and even the periods where discomfort, both physical and emotional, gets intense. Once we have settled into awareness of breath and environment, we rest our mind in the silence—meaning the moment as it is—which has plenty of room for the mental chatter. Remember, though, we enter the silence not by *trying* to enter but simply through the constant, gentle effort to just be here.

Surrendering to the physical experience of breath and environment, we use the experience of sitting still, basically doing nothing, to awaken our sense of what's most real, of what's most important. The dual awareness of breath and environment becomes a doorway or a portal into reality. As long as we live in the bubble of our thoughts and judgments, we cut ourselves off from the mystery of our Being. Yet we can often tap into the mystery through just a quiet presence in the moment. Through watching, and through reflecting without thinking.

Perhaps you have felt a sense of ease when you've allowed yourself to *just be;* but perhaps you've also discovered that it's very difficult to do. Why? Because one of the biggest problems we have as human beings is our overactive minds. We frequently identify with the thinking mind as who we are rather than relating to it as simply a useful part of us. For example, how often do we find ourselves identifying entirely with our thoughts or emotions? The mind is essentially geared toward survival; it relates to experiences as problems to be solved: it analyzes, organizes, makes decisions—all in order to make us feel comfortable and safe. The mind, of which the ego is a part, is basically interested in controlling our experiences, controlling our world. This is not, in itself, a bad thing. In fact, it can help us navigate through the inevitable difficulties we have as human beings.

However, the problem is that the thinking mind takes over and makes our world a protected cocoon—small and narrow—and, as a consequence, we shut life out. We're no longer present to our life. Instead of the presence of just being, we get caught in wanting to feel a particular way, in wanting to *be* a particular way. The mind is zeroed in on wanting to feel safety, security, pleasure, and, perhaps most of all, control. For example, many of us have the deeply seated belief that only by effort and doing can we get what we want. We believe, at least on a subtle level, that we need to push ourselves. We may not like to think of ourselves in this way, but simple observation will show us that we do it all day long. We feel the need to struggle and push, to fix whatever seems to be a problem. This is based in the ideal of being active, of doing, of being productive—all of which require making things happen, making things better. This may be fine and even necessary in some areas of daily life, but when we're struggling to be or feel a particular way, it causes tension and misery.

But there's another kind of effort that's possible for us—a kind of effort that comes more from the heart than from the mind. It involves simply *being* rather than doing; instead of trying to fix or control, the inclination is more toward openness or receptivity. Instead of trying to struggle, the aspiration is to connect. This dynamic is at the heart of meditation practice. For example, what usually happens when we sit down to meditate? When our mind is busy, don't we often think it means that something is wrong? And when we think that something is wrong, don't we usually translate that into the belief that something is wrong with *us?* Furthermore, don't we usually think that we have to *do* something about it? As a consequence we habitually move into the fix-it mode.

But there's an alternative way to approach these so-called problems. No matter what we bring to our meditation, no matter how we may be feeling—either physically or emotionally—the practice is to simply sit down, acknowledge what's going on, and then surrender to what is. We don't need to "let it go"—we simply let it *be* there. What this requires is the basic understanding that our states of body and mind are not problems to be solved or obstacles to be overcome. Just because something seems off doesn't mean that something is, in fact, off. Things simply are what they are. It's primarily our judgments about them—our expectations about how things should be—that cause us endless difficulties.

For example, if we get bored or sleepy during meditation, we often unconsciously judge the experience as a bad sitting period. If we get agitated or upset, we often think that we have to become calm. If we get confused, we search for clarity. But the fact is, no matter what may be occurring, all we need to do is acknowledge what's happening and then be as fully present as we can. The underlying principle is that awareness heals.

So the instruction is to simply let it be. Please be clear: this is *not* a passive or pseudo detachment; we still need the active discipline to stay present, to remain still, and to be precise in our self-observation. But there's a particular attitude of mind/heart that's willing simply to look, to be open to what comes up, to be curious, to cease judging and resisting. And as we learn to cease our resistance to what is, there will be a growing willingness to be with, and perhaps even enjoy on some level, our repeating patterns, our little human dramas, the whole passing show. Eventually, we learn how to surrender to our experience without falling into the trap of wallowing in it.

When we sit down to meditate, anxiety may arise. Certainly resistance and discouragement will also come up. The practice is to see the thoughts, *feel* the physical aspects of anxiety, become aware of the breath and environment, and just let it all *be* there. Whatever our state of mind or body might be, the practice is to really feel what that is; and while staying with the breath and the environment, we let it be as it is. The point is that no matter what we feel, no matter what comes up for us, the practice is to clearly see the believed thoughts, to truly feel and reside in the visceral experience of what is, and then, with the breath and the environmental input as our bigger context, to let our experience just be.

In a way this practice is very simple. But it can also be very difficult to do. Why? Because, again, the mind is simply not inclined to let things be. It does not want to give up its pictures, its opinions, its judgments, of how things should be. It is much more interested in analyzing, judging, blaming, controlling, and, above all, making things "better." But it's possible to understand that in meditation we don't have to *be* some particular way, nor do we have to *feel* any special way. When we truly understand this, we're relieved of a very heavy burden. Cultivating this more spacious sense of awareness, we can begin to open into our sitting and open into our life.

Perhaps the one quality that meditation practice requires most is perseverance. In the long course of our quest for contentment and wisdom, there will no doubt be many ups and downs. There will likely be periods of discouragement, where we don't even remember why we started in the first place. But perseverance allows us to continue with the practice regardless of what mood we're in or how motivated we are in the moment. In my teaching, I emphasize the quality of perseverance more than any other; in fact, one student recently told me that when he thinks of me, he imagines that the first word out of my mouth after I was born was perseverance. But the truth is, it took me many years to cultivate this quality.

We have to keep coming back to the basic understanding: practice is possible in just one place—in residing in exactly what we are experiencing *right now*. It can be very helpful to occasionally ask the three questions from the last chapter: Am I truly happy right now? What blocks happiness? Can I surrender to what is? This is an excellent way of focusing attention on what is going on in the present moment. The last question, in particular, goes to the heart of cultivating both presence and genuine happiness. Surrendering to what is— learning to stay, to persevere—is the key to a lifelong meditation practice. And within that we simply observe whatever arises. Eventually, we may find it possible to do so in a lighter, more playful manner.

Objectively observing whatever arises has been a recurring theme in our discussion of uncovering what blocks genuine happiness and also in cultivating its roots. Observing might sound straightforward, but in reality, we have an uncanny ability to get in our own way. Here's an example: a detective was given three apprentices to train, and his first task was to teach them how to be observant. He showed the first apprentice a photo of a suspect in profile and told the apprentice to look carefully at the image. After several seconds he turned the photo over and asked the apprentice how he would recognize the suspect. The apprentice said, "That's easy—he only has one eye."

The detective was flabbergasted and immediately decided that this apprentice would never be a detective. He called in the second apprentice and showed him the same picture for a few seconds. Then he asked him what he observed that would help him recognize the suspect. The second apprentice answered, "I couldn't miss him—he only has one ear." At this point, the detective became irate. He couldn't believe the two apprentices were so dumb that they didn't know they were looking at a profile.

Finally, the detective called in the third apprentice and again, after briefly showing him the photo, asked him what he observed that would help him recognize the suspect. After a moment, the apprentice answered, "The suspect wears contact lenses." The detective was thrown off guard, and he went to his computer to check on the suspect. He was amazed to find that the suspect did, in fact, wear contact lenses. The detective returned to the third apprentice and told him he was very impressed. He then asked, "How did you make such an acute observation?" The apprentice answered, "That's easy—he can't wear regular glasses because he has only one ear and one eye."

This example is admittedly absurd, but as we observe ourselves long enough, we will see that at times we can be almost equally absurd. Particularly in meditation, eventually *everything* will come up, including the things we haven't wanted to see. Yet, as we persevere with the practice, we can learn to observe our various neuroses and idiosyncrasies without the filter of our judgments; instead, we can view them with a benign tolerance. We can even develop a sense of humor at the absurdity of human behavior, including our own. Learning to be able to laugh at ourselves is one of the many benefits of a meditation practice, and it is also a sign of spiritual maturity. My strong conviction is that cheerful perseverance is one of the keys to a fruitful spiritual life. Once we truly learn this, almost everything is workable in the context of our meditation practice.

The main point is that persevering with a meditation practice is instrumental in experiencing a life of genuine happiness. Learning to reside in the stillness, the silence, of *just being* allows us to taste the sweetness of doing nothing. This is not a state of laziness, where we just lie around feeling pleasure. Hedonism is rarely sweet for very long, for it is rooted in trying to satisfy cravings that can never be completely satisfied. Moreover, when we feed the tendency to crave, we guarantee our continuing unhappiness. The deeper sweetness of doing nothing requires an ability to just be present with ourselves—not trying to do things to stay busy or find pleasure in order to fill up an inner absence. Instead, sitting in meditation allows us to *just be*. This is true even in the midst of discomfort. When we can refrain from the story line of our thoughts—about the past or the future— and instead attend to the immediacy of the physical experience of our life, we can connect with a sense of presence, of openness, that is one of the main roots of genuine happiness.

Basic Meditation Instructions

If possible, it is best to meditate in the same place every day. Ideally, the space should be uncluttered and as quiet as possible.

It is also beneficial to meditate at the same time every day to help foster the discipline necessary to overcome occasional laziness or loss of motivation.

Many people find it helpful to have a small altar. Lighting a candle or a stick of incense can help kindle our aspiration, as can having an inspirational picture or quotation on the altar.

Ideally, you will sit in meditation every day. At the very least, sit three or four times a week. When you first begin your meditation practice, it is okay to sit for just fifteen minutes, but you should gradually increase your time up to thirty or forty minutes.

Whether you sit on a cushion or in a chair, it is helpful to sit in an erect but relaxed posture. Staying erect helps keep the mind alert, while staying relaxed helps prevent unnecessary strain.

The eyes should be open, but looking down slightly. It is best to use "soft" eyes, or peripheral vision, where you're not looking directly at any particular point. The reason the eyes are kept open is that it is too easy to enter into a dreamy state with the eyes closed. This may feel pleasant, but it is not conducive to being awake and aware, which are two of the main points of meditating.

Start by taking a couple of deep breaths to bring awareness into the body.

Then, to help settle the body and mind, bring a focused attention to the breath. Feel the specific physical sensations of the breath entering and leaving the body. For example, you can focus on the area in the center of the chest as the breath goes in and out. Stay present with the physical experience of breathing for as long as you can, being aware of the tendency to have the attention pulled away into thinking, daydreaming, or planning.

During a single sitting period, you may get pulled away into thinking hundreds of times. This is very normal, and there is no need to judge yourself as a bad meditator. Instead, each and every time you catch yourself lost in the mind, simply return to the physical sensations of the breath.

INTERMEDIATE INSTRUCTIONS

In the early stages of a meditation practice, it is fine to follow the breath for the entire sitting period, but as the mind and body begin to feel settled, it is good to let the awareness expand to include other sensations in the body, as well as input from the environment, such as sounds and the texture of the air. This allows us to move from a very concentrated awareness on just the breath to a more open state of awareness. Since thoughts will no doubt continue to arise, the instruction is to notice them and label them if necessary, and then refrain from letting them play out by returning to awareness of the breath and the input from the environment.

When you find yourself caught in thoughts, it is helpful to make the intention to come back to being present for at least the duration of three breaths. The first breath reestablishes awareness of the breath itself; the second reestablishes awareness of the environment; and the third reintroduces an overall awareness of the breath *and* the environment together. Even if you have to come back to these three breaths dozens of times during a sitting period, eventually the dual awareness of breath and environment will become the foundation of your meditation practice.

When emotions arise that demand your attention, instead of trying to ignore them or bypass them, bring awareness to the physical texture of the emotion, but do so within the larger container of awareness of breath and environment.

Students often judge meditation periods as bad if they can't focus, or if they don't feel good. But one of the great benefits of meditation comes from persevering anyway, regardless of how we feel. Eventually, a learning and a settling will begin to take place. And gradually, the sense of presence and equanimity that is cultivated through a daily meditation practice begins to be infused into our everyday living.

9

Gratitude

One of my favorite quotes from the Buddha is: "Let us rise up and be thankful, for if we didn't learn a lot today, at least we learned a little, and if we didn't learn a little, at least we didn't get sick, and if we got sick, at least we didn't die; so, let us all be thankful."

Gratitude is one of the fruits of living from genuine happiness; at the same time, it arises from an inherent seed in our being, a seed that requires cultivation. There's a quote by Meister Eckhart, the Christian mystic, that illustrates how important this quality is: "If the only prayer you said in your whole life was 'thank you,' that would suffice." If we truly understood the depth of this teaching it would be all we'd need to know. Unfortunately, we can't just tell ourselves to be grateful and expect it to happen, yet it's a quality that certainly can be nurtured.

Gratitude is sometimes defined as thankfulness. It's also described as an appreciative attitude in which we acknowledge that something good is happening. But how often do we truly feel grateful? Perhaps we feel it when something really "good" happens, but how grateful are we for the things we consider more neutral or even bad? For example, how grateful are we for something as simple and basic as each breath?

How grateful are we for our capacity for loving-kindness? How grateful are we for our whole journey of awakening, *including* the difficulties?

Gratitude is one of the essential aspects of being truly happy, because if we're not grateful for what we have, we will always want life to be different from what it is—a demand that will surely guarantee our unhappiness. There's a Tibetan slogan that says, "Be grateful to everyone." What is this asking of us—because it clearly sounds unrealistic, if not impossible? Are we supposed to be grateful for our roommate who doesn't clean the sink, or our boss who doesn't appreciate us? Are we supposed to be grateful for someone who criticizes us? Of course we are! Because from the point of view of spiritual practice, *whoever*, or *whatever*, pushes us to our edge— to that place where we're stuck, and beyond which we don't want to go—is our teacher and takes us to the exact place where the deepest learning takes place.

Take the example of the roommate who doesn't clean the sink. Why should we be grateful? Because the roommate is pointing us to exactly where we're stuck—in our anger, in our judgments about how things should be, in our self-righteousness. How about the person who criticizes us? Why should we be grateful? Because the situation gives us the opprtunity to address the hurt and fear that we would probably otherwise ignore—the very hurt and fear that prevent us from experiencing genuine happiness.

Yet, how often do we actually remember this—that these difficult situations are our best teachers? Most of the time we're caught up in believing our own expectations of how life should be, which is one of our prime detours from reality, as well as from genuine happiness. We expect people to appreciate us, save us, or at least not criticize us; we expect that life will go a particular way—with our finances or our health—which guarantees that we'll repeatedly experience disappointment rather than gratitude. In short, when we're caught in the thought-based world of expectations, we will always experience the unhappiness of the thinking mind, which constantly tells us that the present moment is not what it should be.

Practices for Cultivating Gratitude

Though gratitude is an invaluable quality, trying to make it a goal or an ideal to be achieved is rarely helpful. If we tell ourselves we *should* be grateful, we're just creating another mental picture out of which we live, hoping that it will bring us happiness. But chasing after happiness doesn't bring us happiness; it only perpetuates the craving mind and blocks any sense of real appreciation or gratitude for life. It is, however, possible to cultivate gratefulness without making it into an ideal. Here are two practices that I've found very helpful that you might want to try.

Nightly Reflection

Nightly reflection is a relaxed meditation that is done right before going to sleep. I do it lying on my back in bed with my hands folded on my stomach. The eyes can be open or closed. It's best to do this at approximately the same time each night, and it's especially important to do before getting too tired.

The intention of nightly reflection is to recall the main events of the day, starting with the first memory of the morning. During nightly reflection, it's very important not to get pulled into thinking, analyzing, associating, or judging; the reflection is intended to just review—or observe in hindsight, as objectively as possible—what *actually* transpired.

Once the review is finished, you ask yourself the question "What am I most grateful for?" And then the mind can pinpoint those experiences during the day for which you feel appreciation, even though you might not have acknowledged it at the time. By doing the nightly reflection regularly, we not only become more grateful during the meditation itself, but we also become more aware and receptive during the day. For example, we begin to notice that as we go through our daily routine, little positive moments are often not even acknowledged, or if they are, are quickly forgotten. But as we become more attuned to what is actually happening during the day, these moments begin to stand out, and gratitude is more likely to arise in the present moment.

Thich Nhat Hanh, the well-known Vietnamese Zen teacher, speaks about how mindfulness, or awareness in everyday life, can foster gratitude. For example, he points out that when we're aware, we begin to notice even the most simple thing, such as how turning on a faucet brings us water; so instead of taking running water for granted, which most of us do, we instead cultivate awareness and appreciation. After all, having running water is certainly not our birthright; the majority of people throughout history, and many millions even today, do not have this luxury. Awareness allows us to appreciate such things and also to recognize our sense of entitlement; but it is only through intentional practice, such as the practice of reviewing our day each evening, and reflecting on what we're most thankful for, that we actively cultivate the awareness that's necessary to make this type of gratitude a more integral part of everyday living.

A Day of Saying Thank You

Another practice to help cultivate gratitude is to periodically devote a whole day to slowing down and saying "thank you"—three breaths at a time—to *everything* that comes your way, no matter what. The instructions are quite simple: at various points throughout the day, you:

1. Pause—ceasing activity for the duration of just three breaths
2. Breathe—bringing awareness to the center of the chest, feeling the breath.
3. Say "thank you"—opening to *whatever* is present

One of the things that this practice shows us is how many things we're *not* thankful for. Although it may sound counterintuitive, the truth is that every time something irritates us or scares us, or displeases us in some way, we have the opportunity to learn where we place limitations on thankfulness—for example, where we're still stuck in our own expectations.

Sometimes, however, the disappointment of thwarted expectations is so great that thankfulness can elude us entirely. For example, once a young prince was put under an evil spell by a witch. The spell was that he could only speak one word each year. However, if he didn't use his one word during a given year, he could use two words the next year. One day, the prince saw the princess of his dreams and fell madly in love. All he wanted was to go up to her and say "My darling." So he decided to wait two years before speaking to her.

At the end of the two years, he realized he also wanted to say "I love you." This meant waiting another three years, but he was sure it would be worth it. And true enough, after five years, his love was just as strong, and it was clear to him that he wanted to marry her. But to say "Will you marry me" meant he would have to wait four more years.

Finally, at the end of the nine years, the prince happily appeared before the princess, bent down on one knee, and said, "My darling, I love you. Will you marry me?"

The princess looked at him and said, "Excuse me. What did you say?"

When we have expectations, like the prince, where we're very attached to the outcome, disappointment is almost guaranteed, and it would be very hard to tap into gratitude. Granted, most of the time things aren't this extreme, but even in less dire moments, it's sometimes hard to generate gratitude. In addition, I've often been amazed at how many times I've said "thank you" without feeling the least bit grateful. On the other hand, as we do the daylong practice of saying "thank you," even though it's difficult, over time it begins to call forth gratitude from our inner fabric; and as we work with whatever gets in the way of real gratitude, a genuine sense of appreciation tends to come forth naturally. Eventually, being present for three breaths of gratitude begins to feel like a refreshing drink of reality. We also realize that it's possible to feel inwardly grateful (and genuinely happy) even when our outer life is not going well.

These two exercises—nightly reflection and a day of saying "thank you"—allow us to slowly (and, perhaps, begrudgingly) drop the story line of "me," of what I want, so that the wonder and delight of our basic gratitude become a natural part of how we live. We're very good at seeing what's wrong—with others and with ourselves—but these practices allow us to notice increasingly what's right. Having gratitude for being alive—being able to experience an inner delight in the moment—is one of the essential roots of genuine happiness. We can come to understand that genuine happiness can be very ordinary, such as in the little moments of presence when we meet another person with a twinkle in our eye and have a brief taste of human connection.

Making Gratitude a Way of Life

Over time, we can learn to integrate gratitude in subtle ways as a natural part of our daily living. Recently Elizabeth and I took a trip to London and Paris. We wanted a different kind of vacation—more like a personal retreat than a vacation in the normal sense—where we could slow down and go deeper into our own practice, even while in the midst of activity. Although we did many fun things, we stayed away from the usual tourist attractions; rather, we focused on visiting beautiful parks, meditating in old majestic cathedrals, and attending musical performances. These experiences led me to reflect on the fact that we often talk about being present with difficulties, but rarely do we talk about being present when we're really enjoying ourselves.

For example, there are at least three amazing parks in London—the Kensington Gardens, Regent's Park, and especially Kew Gardens. And also, amazing in a different way, are the Luxembourg Gardens in Paris. We spent many hours walking through these parks and gardens, usually going at a slow pace. We would occasionally meditate in silence, but mostly we just took in the beauty—the flowers in bloom, the vast expanses of many shades of green, the trees that almost talk to you. And it occurred to me that the key to being able to feel grateful in those moments is very basic—it's simply about getting out of the head and opening to the rich world of sensory experiences in the environment.

Another example of the inner appreciation that comes when we can be fully present to the external world is in strolling through the streets of Paris, which we both love to do—admiring buildings, checking out people, not going anywhere special, not doing anything special, simply being present to what is here. The key to this kind of appreciation is what the Zen master Suzuki Roshi called beginner's mind, where we simply open ourselves to take in our experience without prejudging or trying to control anything.

One evening in Paris we went swing dancing. The place was a cellar-like cavern, with a little boogie-woogie band. Almost everyone there was quite young, and at first I felt the tinge of self-consciousness trying to take hold, which is all Me stuff, all head stuff. But both of us seemed to be able to drop the whole self-image thing and have a great time simply dancing with each other. We're both pretty good at old-time jitterbugging, but the point isn't that we were good, but rather that we weren't *trying* to be good, not trying to be special, which allowed us to really *be* there. What I'm trying to describe is what it means to bring the mind of meditation into everyday life—to *be* Zen, or appreciate the sweetness of the moment. Being awake and grateful in these daily pleasures is not about an emotional high but instead is more about a sense of presence.

This kind of gratitude includes a bigger sense of reality, which we certainly experienced in the enormous parks and the ancient cathedrals; and along with that we experienced a subtle awareness of the ephemeral nature of things. When we're aware of how quickly life can change—that the ice can crack under our feet at any moment—there is a sense of poignancy for our short time on earth. We often feel this poignancy when someone close to us is gravely ill or dies. But this awareness that life is short does not need to be discouraging or lead to the cynical or bitter conclusion that nothing matters. There's still this very life, however short, *to live*.

It's what we do with the time we have that matters. Living a life that is inherently worthwhile comes from being present to it—from no longer clinging to our protections and pretenses, to our small comforts or fleeting goals. This presence fosters the experience of gratitude for the genuine value of every experience, including those we would normally not think to be grateful for.

For example, I have regular flare-ups of my immune system disorder, so I am particularly grateful when I'm physically able to take walks, cook, or sit cross-legged during meditation—activities that I can't do when I'm not well. But I've also learned to be grateful even during the flare-ups, because often these long periods of quiet and inactivity are the times that I can surrender into and dwell most deeply in the heart. The point is that gratitude can encompass the broad spectrum of human experiences, from the emotional highs of personal happiness to the depth of our suffering, so long as we are open to the present moment.

There is no harm in enjoying personal happiness for what it is, but it's important not to confuse personal happiness with the deeper or more genuine happiness of true contentment—

a happiness that is not based on favorable external circumstances. In fact, the enjoyment that we feel in moments of personal happiness is appreciated even more when we are more awake, more present. These are the rich quiet delights of being *here*, when life feels vivid and sometimes even luminous. Yet when we're blindly caught up, even in pleasure, where there is not a sense of presence, the wonder and gratitude can easily be missed.

It is certainly true that gratitude can come forth naturally when we are happy; in this sense it is an integral part of the experience of happiness. But it is also true that we can consciously cultivate gratitude as one of the basic roots of genuine happiness, no matter what the external circumstances of our lives may be. Using tools such as a nightly reflection practice or a day of saying "thank you," in conjunction with other awareness practices, can help bring gratitude to our daily lives; and as it becomes increasingly possible for us to experience gratitude, we will find that true happiness flows forth naturally.

Part Three

Cultivating Happiness

GIVING FROM THE HEART

10

Generosity of the Heart

Many years ago I heard a proverb that went something like this:

If you want to be happy for an hour, eat a good meal;
If you want to be happy for a day, make love;
If you want to be happy for a year, get married;
If you want to be happy for a lifetime, live an honest life.

I didn't find the last line quite satisfying, so for several weeks I reflected on it, questioned it, wrestled with it, until one day the answer I was looking for came to me: "If you want to be happy for a lifetime, give yourself to others."

Living mainly to get something for ourselves is a prime source of our unhappiness. The alternative is to give from the generosity of the heart. When we truly offer ourselves to someone in need—whether they are hungry or sick or deprived in some way—we experience the gratitude of living from the awakened heart, and we feel the fulfillment of acting from a sense of our basic connectedness. By contrast, when we give with the expectation of getting something back, it's an immediate setup for disappointment or anger—reactions that ultimately lead to unhappiness.

A line from Ernest Hemingway's *A Farewell to Arms* has stayed with me for many years: "Love is the wanting to do things for." Our deepest happiness comes when we live from this place, attending not only to ourselves but to the welfare of others. Yet paradoxically, even though we know we are happier when we do things for others, research shows that when we're given the choice between doing something self-serving and doing something altruistic, more often than not we will choose the self-centered alternative. Sadly, as this research shows, we don't always do what makes us happy. Even though the deepest happiness comes from giving, most of the time, as we focus on the self-centered pursuit of our own happiness, we continue to feel separate and defended, thus guaranteeing our unhappiness.

It often takes a large dose of disappointment from living a self-centered life to awaken our desire for the happiness of others. But once it is activated, giving from this natural generosity allows us to move out of our chronic state of separateness into a sense of connection with others. Giving from the generosity of the heart is an essential root of the genuine happiness of true contentment.

Often, though, it is not so clear how to give from the natural generosity of the heart. In the early 1990s I was flying home from a meditation retreat, and as the sunlight came through the window of the plane, I was literally flooded with a deep sense of clarity and peace. The experience was noteworthy not so much because it was pleasant but because it was accompanied by a "voice" that told me, "You need to take a step—stop holding yourself back in fear!" I didn't question where these words came from; I just knew somehow that they were true. What I *didn't* know was what to do next, so I tucked the "message" in the back of my mind and waited. Within a few weeks, the hospice organization where I volunteered asked me to lead a meditation-based group on how to deal with burnout. I was not yet a Zen teacher, so this was a big step for me at the time, primarily because my own insecurities made me hesitant to come out of my protected cocoon. However, it was also very clear that this was the exact direction I needed to take.

When the eight-week program I was teaching ended, I started a long-term meditation group for those who wanted to continue. Once again, I had to work with my own anxieties and self-doubts, even though my teacher at the time confirmed my decision and authorized me to teach. In retrospect, I believe I would have done it even without the authorization, for it was clear to me that I had something to offer, and the only thing holding me back was fear.

There are many different ways to give. We can volunteer to help out in any number of situations. We can give through social and political action. And we can certainly learn to give of ourselves at work, in our relationships, or in other facets of the daily life we already have. Giving can be as simple as letting someone get in front of you in line or taking on a chore that normally you would want to avoid, because you see that your partner or roommate is tired. Or perhaps it might involve sitting with a total stranger who is bedridden with terminal illness. The problem isn't finding ways to give; the problem is that we constantly have to deal with the many barriers that inevitably arise in our own minds as we begin to live from the generosity of the heart.

When we see others in need, there may be an instinctive desire to help, but the natural generosity of the heart can be overridden in a microsecond by the mind. The fear-based thinking mind raises doubts: "I don't know what to do" or "I can't get involved." The heart that wants to reach out can easily be closed down by fear or self-protection. For example, we may fear failure or rejection. Or we may be blocked in our desire to give by our own laziness—not wanting to leave the comfort of the familiar. Perhaps most often we get caught in our negative self-judgments, believing that we're not enough.

These judgments limit us and hold us back, even when we feel the sincere desire to give. Even the belief "I'm not a giving person" may be enough to prevent our innate generosity from coming forth.

Our inherent wish to give can also be undermined by unconscious agendas, such as wanting to get something in return. For example, many people volunteer at places like hospice or veterans groups because they want to find a sense of connection, assuage feelings of guilt, or increase their feelings of self-esteem. Even though giving to get may feel good superficially and can motivate us initially, it is never genuinely satisfying, and we miss the natural happiness that results from giving without self-centered agendas.

The real key to being happy for a lifetime is to give oneself to others, like a white bird in the snow. When we're truly generous, we blend in with what's going on. This means giving to others without ulterior motives or a sense of self-importance. We're not drawing attention to ourselves, and our giving isn't just another way of propping up our self-image. Giving ourselves to others, but like a white bird in the snow, means we're able to drop our agendas, including being motivated by the idea that we *should* be more giving.

Obstacles to Genuine Giving

Perhaps the most frequent barrier to true giving is when we give in order to feel appreciated. I had a friend who used to volunteer at a charity for the homeless. We met for coffee one day, and he looked decidedly unhappy. He reported that he was through helping the homeless, and when I asked him if something had happened, he said, "Remember that guy I took to the hospital last month, and then gave him a blanket so he could stay warm on the streets? Well, I ran into him today a few blocks from here, and he spit on me and told me to get the hell out of his way." My friend and I talked about this a bit more, and finally he said, "You know, I realize I just wanted him to thank me, to appreciate me." I imagine that every one of us can relate to this feeling. When our motivation for helping is to fill our *own* needs—whether that need be appreciation, validation, worth, or something else—it's bound eventually to lead to dissatisfaction.

Another detour off the path of giving from the generosity of the heart is when we take on the identity of "helper." Sometimes, when a friend, or even someone we hardly know, is having a difficult time, we feel the natural urge to help. But we can easily get sidetracked by falling into the helping or fix-it mode. If the situation is painful, we often look for something concrete to *do* in an attempt to try to make the problem go away. But by being active, by "doing," we may really be trying to avoid our *own* discomfort or feeling of helplessness. I remember when a hospice patient died while I was in the home. I was all too happy to "help" by running errands and going to the store for the spouse. But when I got back, it was clear to me that I was "helping" as a means to avoid facing the discomfort that came up for me in the situation. This was a detour from genuine giving, and once I saw this, I stayed with the family and simply offered my presence without trying to do anything special.

When we experience discomfort in the face of our own difficult situations or another person's suffering, of course it is understandable to resist or turn away. We instinctively fear the unknown; we feel dread in moving toward the sense of groundlessness that is inherent in such situations. But the generosity of the heart tugs at us and reminds us not to hold back—it reminds us to instead say "yes" to our experience by intentionally moving toward it. Only by opening to our own fears and letting them in can we begin to explore the unknown territory where all real learning takes place. As soon as we acknowledge our fears about giving, we take the first step away from their grip. Awareness is the beginning of the healing process. And even when we take an inevitable step backward into our old patterns, and are once more caught in the same dark places, at least we know that daylight is possible.

We have to remember that in working with whatever blocks our innate generosity we're not trying to destroy the ego; the ego actually plays an important role in our ability to do good. However, what's necessary is to decrease our identification with the conditioned, self-centered Me and to simultaneously increase our identification with the aspiration to live in a more awake, life-centered manner—that is, directly from the heart. As we work with our conditioning and our fears, the generosity of the heart gradually flows forth naturally—we don't even have to think about it.

If we reflect on what it means to give from the heart, at some point it becomes clear that giving may first mean *giving up*—giving up our strong identification with being only our small self, our separate self. This is the self of judgments and fears; it's the self that holds back the natural inclination to give, either through laziness, a sense of entitlement, self-doubt, or the need for appreciation or self-esteem. But as we work with this little self by repeatedly bringing awareness to it, it starts to lose its power; gradually we find it becomes easier for us to extend the natural generosity of the heart. In some situations, this may mean giving money or material goods. As this generosity evolves, it will mean giving our attention and presence. Ultimately it means giving our heart.

Helping Others by Just Being Present

Sometimes we will discover that giving doesn't seem to produce tangible results. For example, when we genuinely extend ourselves to others who are feeling alone and isolated in their pain, we may be able to do very little to take away their suffering. But in some cases, it's enough to let another person know that someone cares, and at the very least they know that they are not alone. When we drop our pretenses and the need to be a "helper" or someone special, we can simply be present with someone in their suffering. A bond arises, and the other may know, even if it's not conscious, that we're there with them—with an unspoken connection of the heart.

Then there are those times when there's nothing we can give or do that makes even this small relief possible. It can be very painful to see that even our best efforts sometimes don't seem to bring any positive change. We may end up judging ourselves mercilessly for not being caring enough or worthy enough. We may see ourselves as weak, or ineffective, or lacking in compassion. We may feel discouragement or even anger that the person "rejected" our kindness, our help. In these moments, it is helpful to breathe our own painful experience directly into the center of the chest, and extend loving-kindness not only to the other in their pain but also to ourselves in our discouragement, in our anger, in our frustration. This compassion toward the whole situation allows us to continue; and eventually we can tap into the profound sense of connection and gratitude that comes when we can once again offer the generosity of the heart, regardless of the outcome.

As a teacher I often witness students being stuck in their conditioning and fears. Sometimes I feel the urge to give them strong encouragement to move forward. But remembering how much patience is required reminds me not to underestimate how difficult it may be for others to move through their own stuck places. When I remember this, I can then simply *be* with them, regardless of where they are in their own process. What we can give in these situations is patience and empathy. Maybe only a few words are all that is needed—whatever flows naturally from an understanding heart. When we have genuine empathy for what another is experiencing, they can feel heard, feel understood; and thus they can experience the healing touch of human-to-human connection.

There are other kinds of situations where giving may require something more concrete than just being empathetic. For example, when we're faced with social and political injustice, we may be called to take action in order to address the injustice. But even when our intentions are sincere, we have to be especially mindful not to let our actions be poisoned with the toxicity of anger. It may be natural to experience anger in certain situations, but acting from that anger is likely to bring the opposite results from what we intend or desire. Acting from anger means we're caught in closed-heartedness—a guarantee that our wish to live from genuine happiness will be undermined.

Anger can, however, be transformed into *resolve*, making it possible to act from an inner sense of peace instead of letting our angry actions sabotage our best intentions. This may require first sitting with our anger in the stillness and silence of meditation for as long as it takes to move out of our closed-heartedness.

Most of all we have to remember that the basic source and foundation of our efforts to give—whether at home, in volunteering, or in social action—is the awakened heart. Unless we are in contact with this source, our efforts will take us on a detour away from our original intentions and may well be fed by anger and fear instead of by our innate generosity.

To live from the generosity of the heart does not require following any particular course of action, such as having a special job, being a volunteer, or engaging in social or political change. If we remain open to the unknown, and are willing to decline fear's call when it tries to pull us back into protection, we become available to follow the natural inclination of the heart to give in even the smallest ways and under the most unlikely circumstances. We can always ask ourselves, "What can I give?" For example, when we see a homeless person, along with offering them money, we can also give them the warmth of our heart by looking into their eyes without judgment. When we see a fellow passenger struggling with their luggage, we can reach out and offer a hand, even if it slows us down or is inconvenient. When we hear about the many thousands of children who suffer and die each day because they don't have enough to eat, we can immediately go online and make a donation to help feed the hungry, even if it means facing our own fears that we may not have enough. Whether or not we have enough money to give, the one thing we can always do is visualize those who are suffering from hunger and breathe their image into the center of the chest on the inbreath, and on the outbreath extend compassion for their plight.

The point is, no matter how we give of ourselves, whether in very small or grand ways, whether in material or intangible forms, doing so without pretense cultivates our innate generosity; and little by little, the natural expression of our basic connectedness evolves. Giving on this level—from our true openhearted nature—is one of the essential roots of a life of true contentment.

11

Loving-Kindness

I've been teaching Zen for many years to students from around
the world, and although no two students are exactly the same,
there are often common threads. In fact, one thing that has
become abundantly clear to me is that the tendency to judge
ourselves negatively, to see ourselves as lacking in some fundamental way, is one of the primary causes of unhappiness.
This is why it's critically important to discover what undercuts the solidity of our negative self-judgments and to learn
to live more from the awakened heart of loving-kindness. We
have to find out what it takes to stop living from the fear of
not measuring up, the fear of being nothing, the fear of being
unworthy of love.

A student recently came to talk to me about her struggles
with her Zen practice. She was feeling alone, ashamed, and
afraid. I'd known her for a long time and was very fond of her,
but I realized that no matter how much I appreciated her, or
no matter how much I tried to be helpful to her with sugges-
tions on what to do, there was no way I could take away her
suffering. She had to do that herself. In moments like these,
when I realize there is very little I can do to help, I try to
remember to take a few deep breaths into the heart. So with
this particular student, I simply breathed her suffering in and

extended to her the wish that she be healed in her difficulty. In this instance, it was very clear that she was caught in her ego-mind, the mind that feels ashamed and afraid and judges ourselves negatively. This is the mind that limits us and causes us so much unhappiness.

My wish for everyone, when they are hurting, frightened, or berating themselves for not being good enough, is to re-member to bring the quality of loving-kindness to their ex-perience. For example, with this student, I suggested that she take a few breaths into the heart, breathing her suffering right in, and extending to herself the same kindness that she would extend to someone she truly cared about.

It's important to understand that the heart of loving-kindness *is* who we are; it is the nature of our Being. It's equally important that we learn how to extend loving-kind-ness toward ourselves, just as we do for others. As we practice loving-kindness, it becomes a means by which we learn to awaken the heart and embrace our true nature. There is an interesting dynamic between loving-kindness and happiness: loving-kindness tends to come forth naturally as we increas-ingly live a life of genuine happiness; at the same time, as we nurture loving-kindness directly, it cultivates the roots of true contentment.

The essence of the loving-kindness practice is to give: to actively give unconditional friendliness, both to ourselves and others. It's the natural expression of the generosity of the heart. It's about cultivating an attitude of mind in which we desire the welfare of everyone. With loving-kindness, we ex-perience a sense of connectedness, of innate goodwill, perhaps accompanied by receptivity and warmth. Loving-kindness practice also helps us refrain from being caught in the judg-mental mind. There is a sense of openness that diminishes the mind's tendency to constantly judge. In the practice of loving-kindness we no longer push away aspects of ourselves (or oth-ers) that we normally judge as unwanted or bad.

In traditional loving-kindness practice, often referred to as *metta* practice, the emphasis is usually on trying to generate the feeling of loving-kindness by repeating phrases like "May I be happy" and "May all beings be happy." The point is to cultivate a compassionate attitude of mind, which is an essential part of the Buddhist tradition. The approach here will be a little different; instead of trying to generate a particular feeling, such as feeling loving or kind, the emphasis will be on relating to how we are right now, but with heartfelt friendliness. If we are feeling closed-hearted, such as when we're angry or fearful, the practice is to bring awareness into the center of the chest via the inbreath, and on the outbreath to extend the wish that we (or others) be healed in that very difficulty.

Staying with the physical experience of the breath into the area of the heart not only keeps us grounded in physical reality, it also undercuts the forcefulness and solidity of the judgmental mind. This allows us to access our natural capacity to be open, to relate with a deep sense of friendliness to ourselves and to others, exactly as we are.

For the past fifteen years, I've done the loving-kindness meditation every day. As part of the meditation, I often bring to mind people who have died that I was once close to—people who represent something I want to remember. For example, one of these people was a hospice patient who was around my age at the time I met her. She was dying of cancer, but even though she knew her days were limited, she still couldn't ask her daughters or husband to do things for her because she feared inconveniencing them. One time she couldn't even ask for a glass of milk because her deeply ingrained self-judgment was that she didn't count and shouldn't be a bother. It was very sad to witness, and yet there was nothing I could do about it. So when I remember her during my meditation, as someone I cared about, I also remember her fear, her fear of being unworthy, and it still inspires me to be aware of my own limiting self-judgments. It reminds me to extend loving-kindness to myself and, instead of judging, to live more from the heart.

Although loving-kindness is a natural quality of our true nature, it does not usually come forth readily—especially when we get caught in self-criticism, in seeing ourselves as a failure, or as not "enough" in some fundamental way. This is normally a very dark and unhappy place, and rarely do we even think to extend kindness to ourselves. Our self-judgments are often so incessant that there is little room for mercy. That is why it is necessary to cultivate the practice of loving-kindness on a regular basis, so we can tap into it when we are caught in the solidity of the self-judgmental mind. Practicing the loving-kindness meditation regularly helps activate the unconditional friendliness and warmth of the heart, including those times when self-judgment is strongest.

As we cultivate the quality of loving-kindness, we no longer view ourselves as defective. When our conditioning arises and we get caught in old patterns, like anger or fear, instead of regarding them as flaws, we see them simply as old conditioning. Perhaps we learn to say, "Here it is again—I wonder what it will feel like this time?"—and then return to bodily awareness. Thus, with curiosity and kindness (and maybe even a little humor), we replace the heavy burden of being a "Me" with the lightness of heart that is an essential ingredient of genuine happiness.

Cultivating loving-kindness toward ourselves also opens the heart to others. As we enter into our own painful experiences and truly reside in them, without indulging our melodramatic stories; and as we extend loving-kindness to ourselves in our pain, we naturally develop the heartfelt capacity to feel empathy and loving-kindness toward others who are also caught in pain. We understand that we are no different from others—that their pain is no different from our pain. This is not an intellectual understanding; it is an understanding of the heart—one that comes from the courage to truly stay present with our own pain. However, this ability to stay present and bring loving-kindness to our experience takes practice, and to be most effective, one should practice regularly. The instructions that follow describe very specifically how to do the loving-kindness meditation.

LOVING-KINDNESS MEDITATION

Either sitting in meditation posture or lying in a comfortable position, begin by taking a couple of deep breaths. Become aware of the breath and begin to follow it into the center of the chest, relaxing into the body. Experience the area around the heart. Whatever you feel, just be aware of that. With each inbreath let awareness go a little deeper.

To activate the quality of loving-kindness, first think of someone for whom you have very positive feelings. Picture them. Breathe them in. Let your innate loving-kindness be activated.

TO ONESELF

Now shift the focus to yourself, and stay with each of the following lines for a few breaths.

Breathing in, dwelling in the heart.
Breathing out, extending loving-kindness to myself, exactly as I am right now.

Relate with a benign friendliness to wherever you may be caught in your conditioning, including the self-judgments of being flawed or lacking. If there is no warmth, no loving-kindness to extend, simply notice this, and continue.

Breathing in, dwelling in the heart.
Breathing out, there's no one special to be.

Feel the momentary freedom of no longer living from pretense or images of how you should be or feel, including the need to feel special, or loving.

Breathing in, dwelling in the heart.
Breathing out, just Being.

Drop the need to struggle, to get somewhere, to prove yourself; feel the spaciousness and lightness of heart of living from our natural Being.
Repeat the above lines two more times.

To Others

Now think of someone close to you, for whom you wish to extend loving-kindness. Breathe the person's image into the center of the chest on the inbreath. On the outbreath extend loving-kindness to this person while repeating the following three lines. If you feel resistance, just acknowledge it and experience whatever is in the way.

Breathing [name] in,
May you dwell in the heart.

Breathing [name] in,
May you be healed in your difficulties.

Breathing [name] in,
May your heart be open to others.

Repeat these lines inserting the names of any other people you'd like to include in this meditation.

To Everyone

Finally, expand awareness to include everyone. Bring this awareness into the center of the chest with the inbreath, and with the outbreath repeat these three lines, allowing loving-kindness to be extended to everyone.

Breathing everyone in,
May you dwell in the heart.

Breathing everyone in,
May you be healed in your difficulties.

Breathing everyone in,
May your hearts be open to others.

To End

Repeat the first line of this practice, "Breathing in, dwelling in the heart," relaxing into the heartfelt sense of just Being.

Notes on Loving-Kindness Meditation

Cultivating loving-kindness goes against the grain of our habitual patterns, so it is important to do the loving-kindness meditation regularly. Sometimes devoting a whole day to practicing loving-kindness can be very instructive.

Some students say that this meditation is too complicated, that there are too many lines to remember; however, those who are sincere about their practice seem to find ways to adapt the lines yet maintain the spirit of the meditation.

The lines in the loving-kindness meditation are not the same as affirmations. Affirmations are often used to change our feelings or circumstances, whereas the lines of the loving-kindness meditation are not about changing anything; they're about experiencing whatever is present within the spaciousness of the heart.

The first few times you do the loving-kindness meditation you might feel awkward or strange silently repeating the words to yourself. You may also experience discomfort while breathing in and out of the center of the chest in such a focused way. However, no matter what your experience—whether it be awkwardness, judgment, skepticism, or something else—it is well worth it to stay with the practice. I don't know of any other practice that's as effective in undercutting the perniciousness of the judgmental mind or in helping us break through our chronic state of separateness. There is a power beyond words—a power that can't be denied—in breathing in and out of the center of the chest, and incorporating the loving-kindness meditation regularly into our practice life allows us to tap into this power.

Some people feel threatened by the openness of the loving-kindness meditation and react with resistance or even contempt. Many also feel that they're deceiving themselves—that perhaps their experience of loving-kindness is false. Even if you believe these negative thoughts, does this necessarily mean they are true? Of course not! It's just that we believe them. The more you can avoid getting caught in your judgments, the more you will remain open to what is of value.

As we practice loving-kindness on a regular basis, it is no longer just a meditation exercise. It becomes a part of our being, our natural response to life. And whenever we feel stuck, we can remember to simply take a few breaths into the heart.

12

Giving through Work

We spend a large portion of our day, and consequently a large portion of our life span, engaged in our work—whether we work outside the home or as stay-at-home parents. Yet, even though we spend a significant portion of our lives working, how many people are genuinely happy with what they're doing? I don't know what the actual statistics are, but it seems that almost everybody complains about work; very rarely do people look forward to their jobs as a source of genuine happiness.

Unhappiness in our job is often a result of the personal baggage we bring to the situation. For example, if our strategy in life is to try harder and harder, to prove our own worth, we will remain caught on the treadmill of pushing ourselves in order to achieve success as a way to demonstrate our value. But even if we're successful, there's still an underlying fear of being judged as unworthy—and until this fear is addressed, we will remain chronically anxious and unhappy. The same is true with the strategy of trying to please others. Being motivated by the need for approval, and anxiety about possible disapproval, causes an underlying nervous jangle that guarantees our unhappiness, no matter how well we do in our job or how much approval we receive.

Even when we have a strong natural drive to be productive, which can be very fulfilling, our personal baggage easily undermines any sense of satisfaction. For example, the desire for status, or to outdo a coworker, muddies the natural fulfillment of being productive or creative, and again, results in ongoing unhappiness in our work. Yet, even though our life strategies clearly don't bring us happiness, we hold on to them with a stubbornness that defies common sense.

Our strategies to seek happiness through work may sound somewhat crazy, especially since they clearly don't pay off; but we *are* pretty crazy, and we contort reality in crazy ways. In short, we're human! There's a joke about a man who tries on a suit in a custom clothing store, and he says to the tailor, "This one sleeve needs to be shortened—it's two inches too long." The tailor says, "No, all you have to do is bend your elbow like this. See how it makes the sleeve just right." The man replies, "Okay, but when I bend my elbow my collar rises up too high." The tailor says, "No big deal, just hold your head up and back like so." The man says, "But now look how the right shoulder is three inches lower than the left one." The tailor replies, "That's easy—just bend at the waist, over to the right, and you look perfect."

The man walks out of the store wearing the suit, with his elbow bent and out, his head up and back, and his waist bent. The only way he can walk is in a spastic, herky-jerky gait. Two men are walking by and one says, "See how deformed that man is. I sure feel sorry for him." The other man replies, "Yeah, but he must have a terrific tailor—that suit fits him perfectly!"

We don't have to keep contorting or tailoring ourselves to make life fit. The alternative is to first clearly see what we're up to, and then address the beliefs and fears that drive our counterproductive behaviors. Once we begin to work through our layers and layers of personal baggage, reality seems to fit much better.

In a way, the personal baggage that feeds our unhappiness at work has very little to do with the job itself. Changing jobs would not necessarily help, because we would bring the same baggage and anxieties with us. But one very effective way to interrupt this pattern is to ask the three questions about happiness. The first question—Am I truly happy right now?—can help us identify how we're *actually* feeling, because often we don't know. The second question—What blocks happiness?—can specifically clarify where we're acting from fear, such as the fear of being judged as unworthy or the fear of disapproval. The third question—Can I surrender to what is?—helps us to welcome the experience of anxiety, reminding us to breathe the physical sensations of anxiety right into the center of the chest. Based on the fundamental principal that awareness heals, the experience of anxiety becomes much less solid as we learn to welcome it and rest in it. Again, we are not trying to change the experience or to get rid of the anxiety; we are simply welcoming it and letting it be there, just as it is.

Yet, even as we become more free of our anxieties and personal baggage, it's important to seek out work that suits our personality, temperament, and life interests. No matter how much we engage in spiritual practice, certain jobs will be a better fit for us than others. But how do we decide on the best possible job or occupation, and how do we make the choice if our desired job pays very little? Often this is a daunting task; and unfortunately, we usually approach this task by only using the logical or thinking mind, weighing and measuring our options in the hope of finding clarity. This approach may be useful at times, but it will never help us contact what is closest to the heart. Pascal said, "The heart has reasons of which the mind knows nothing," which reminds us of the limitations of the thinking mind. So what are we to do? How do we get in touch with the innermost wisdom of the heart?

When I was in my midtwenties, I was feeling distraught

about finding a suitable occupation. Although I was a successful computer programmer, I knew this didn't resonate with the still, small voice within that was making its presence felt, and I experienced a deep and pervasive anxiety over ever finding the "right" occupation. At the time I was just beginning a spiritual practice, and someone I trusted told me to stop thinking about what to do; instead, whenever the anxiety arose, I was to stay fully present with the anxiety itself. I didn't understand this approach at the time, nor did I find it easy to stay with the physical feelings of anxiety. But I was desperate, so for several weeks I worked on the practice as best I could. Then one day, completely out of the blue, it became crystal clear that my path was to become a carpenter. For a 120-pound intellectual with absolutely no carpentry skills, this was more than a leap—it was ridiculous! But the decision was so clear to me that it led to an unshakable resolve, and in spite of many roadblocks, I pursued this goal. In the end, I experienced a very long and satisfying career as a carpenter and building contractor.

The point is, my decision did not come from thinking; it came from staying present with the anxiety and doubt of not knowing. The problem is we are very hesitant to abandon the thinking mind; we want so badly to believe in the false sense of control that arises when we think we've figured things out. But in looking for the right job or occupation, what serves us better is to practice patience—staying fully present with the experience of not knowing. This is especially true because the thinking mind often asks the wrong questions. We usually want to know what we'll get from the job, but ironically, genuine happiness through our work comes from *giving*, not from what we *get*.

What Do You Have to Offer?

Although happiness naturally arises when we serve others, how often do we think to ask the question "What do I have to offer?" I'm not talking about giving from the ideal that we *should* be giving. Giving from ideals, or from the expectation of some reward, often leads to anger and resentment—and is very different from offering our unique contribution. I'm talking about giving from the heart, without the expectation of getting something in return.

There's a true story about a garbage collector in northern California. As he made his rounds, he regularly waved hello to people in the neighborhood, and he would also try to be very quiet in the morning so he wouldn't disturb anyone. He even used his own money to paint his garbage truck a pleasant color. He became so popular that at one point a petition was started to elect him mayor. But when he heard about it he immediately put a stop to it, saying that all he wanted was to do his best at collecting garbage. In giving what he had to offer and making his best efforts to serve people's needs, he apparently experienced the fulfillment and happiness that come from this kind of selfless giving.

Giving what we have to offer does not necessarily always look like giving. After I worked for many years as a carpenter, I became a building contractor, and for over fifteen years I ran a small construction company specializing in custom homes. For the last several years that I worked there, my practice was to make an effort to bring a harmonious environment to my construction sites. This started when an owner said to me, "This may be the only house I ever build, and I'd like this to be a really good experience, not the nightmare type of experience I often hear about." This led me to reflect on what I could do to not only build a good house but also do it in a way that created a positive experience for everyone involved, from the owner to the lowest-paid laborer.

Most of the workers knew nothing of my meditation practice, and I certainly didn't try to teach them to meditate. But part of my practice was treating everyone equally and never hollering at anyone, even when the job was not done the way I wanted. And when others expressed their negativity, I did what I could to defuse it. For example, sometimes owners and subcontractors would get into a quarrel, so I made a practice of sitting them down together and having each of us agree to pay a third of the cost to remedy what was wrong. This way no one felt they were being taken advantage of, and it also helped make the jobsite a more harmonious place to work.

The sense of value or satisfaction for me in my work as a contractor came not only from being a good builder, technically speaking, but also from bringing my understanding and experience as a meditator into the often messy and complex world of human interactions, trying as much as possible to find ways to create a harmonious environment for everyone.

In asking ourselves what we have to offer, the answer may not be readily apparent. The point is that each of us has our own unique contribution to make. Everyone can't pursue the explicitly altruistic path of helping others, for example, by being a teacher or a social worker. However, even in the business world, which is stereotypically regarded as cutthroat, it can be very satisfying to learn to dedicate our energy to improving the overall work environment. For others, a deeper happiness might arise through offering insight, warmth, or other interpersonal skills, as a way of fostering more sanity and lightheartedness in a workplace that might otherwise seem cold and impersonal. Another's contribution could simply be making his or her best effort to do a good job each day. For example, I once got to know a young woman who worked at Starbuck's; she always greeted me with a warm smile and a friendly word. When I asked her if she was ever in a bad mood, she replied, "Of course, but my calling is to bring good cheer to my customers, which I can't do if I obsess about myself."

Each of us has to reflect on what we have to offer, as well as on what is needed. It may take a while to find our own calling, but this is a very different path from our usual self-centered pursuits in the workplace. When we do our work primarily for money, or to achieve higher status, we're unlikely to find genuine fulfillment. What's missing is the sense of valuing the possibilities available through our work. We often forget that meaning is not inherent in any job. For example, being a doctor is no more inherently meaningful than being a janitor. In fact, many doctors burn out because their expectations of what they'll get for themselves—money, status, appreciation—don't deliver their promise, even when conventional success is achieved.

On the contrary, a study of janitors at a large hospital showed that those who saw themselves as part of the hospital team experienced genuine fulfillment, because they thought more about the welfare of others than about meeting their own self-centered demands. Even though their time was spent emptying bedpans and mopping floors, they went out of their way to contribute, sometimes doing extra tasks to help ease the burdens of the doctors and nurses. As in the example of the garbage collector, they found value in their work by making their best effort to serve others. They also experienced the satisfaction of seeing themselves as contributing to the overall healing environment of the hospital.

Finding happiness through our work requires two basic things. First, we have to recognize our own patterns, such as trying ever harder to be appreciated or doing whatever it takes to get approval. These patterns block any chance of experiencing genuine happiness. And second, once we recognize those patterns, we have to undertake the basic, blue-collar work of practice—the mundane everyday efforts of bringing awareness to the underlying fears that dictate how we feel and act. There is nothing romantic or magical about our blue-collar efforts; they are bound to take time and perseverance, and we may become frustrated at times along the way. But we can remind ourselves regularly that awareness is what ultimately heals.

In addition to staying present with our experience, we can also turn our whole approach toward our work right-side up. We do this by turning away from our normal orientation of "What's in it for me?" and instead ask the question "What do I have to offer?" When we learn to give from our own unique gifts, we can experience the deep fulfillment of living a life in which we prioritize giving over getting. We will also discover that giving from the generosity of the heart is one of the essential roots of true contentment.

13

Giving through Relationships

We often look to relationships as a source of our personal happiness. Our relationships with our partners, friends, and family can certainly be enjoyable, and they enrich many dimensions of living. However, much of our unhappiness in life also comes from relationships; and strangely, even though relationships play a huge role in our lives, we are often very much in the dark when it comes to knowing why so much unhappiness is associated with them. Nor do we have a clear idea what to do about it.

Many books have been written on how to be happy in relationships. They often focus on how to find the right person, communicate better, get our needs met, or fix our problems. Some of these techniques are no doubt helpful, but they are still about striving for personal happiness, where we are at the mercy of external conditions and where we tend to stay caught in the highs and lows of emotion and attachment. And while this may be hard to accept, the personal happiness that we feel periodically through relationships, however enjoyable and meaningful it may be, is usually based in self-centered agendas. This means that we will rarely find the deeper and more genuine happiness that is possible for us.

Conversely, genuine happiness in relationships comes forth naturally when it's no longer blocked by all the conditions that we normally add—our agendas, our needs, our expectations. When we're more able to refrain from indulging our self-centered motivations, we no longer look at our relationships in terms of what we will get. Instead, as we move toward the generosity of the heart, we naturally want to give. Hemingway got it right when he said that "love is the wanting to do things for." The problem is, this is far from easy; relationships are often so complex and messy, and our behaviors are so deeply rooted in our conditioning, that it takes more than the ideal of giving to get us out of our ruts and allow relationships to serve as a fruitful path to true contentment.

Before we explore what it means to give in relationships, let's first look at what relationships are usually about. We always enter into relationships with expectations of what the relationship will do for us. This is true not only in romantic relationships but also in other areas—family, work, friends, and even casual encounters. More often than not, we're not even aware of our expectations; but when we experience a relationship difficulty or conflict, it's likely that our expectations are not being met. (I'm not referring to difficulties that may involve physical danger but rather the garden-variety things that come up in relationships.)

More specifically, whenever we enter into a relationship— from the most casual to the most intense—we want the other person to be a particular way, such as supportive, appreciative, affectionate, trustworthy, or kind. Or perhaps we want them to be neat or quiet. The point is, we *always* have our own agenda about how the other should be. Why? The reason we want the other to be a particular way comes down to the crucial fact that *we* want to feel a particular way; we want to feel safe, secure, appreciated, listened to, in control, and on and on.

When our expectations aren't met, difficulties automatically arise and we may experience disappointment, anger, or fear. Think of a recent conflict in a relationship, and reflect on what expectations you brought with you. See if you're aware of how you wanted the other to be or how you wanted them to make you feel. A helpful question to ask when it's hard to see our own expectations is: "How is it (or he or she) supposed to be?"

Unfortunately, instead of looking inward to see our own expectations, we usually focus on who we can blame or how we can fix the situation. We'll almost always view our relationship difficulties as problems to be solved, as obstacles to overcome. This may work in the short run, and we may be able to temporarily iron out our conflicts and feel some degree of stability. But this approach will never lead to the deeper equanimity of genuine happiness, because we're missing the pivotal understanding that these difficulties, even though they may feel uncomfortable, are *not* problems to be solved. Rather, these difficulties are our *exact path* to freedom, in that they push us to go deeper into our life, to work with the very things that cause us so much unhappiness, namely, our demands that life, and others, be a particular way, and the sense of entitlement we have in thinking that we need to feel a particular way.

Experiencing the disappointment of not getting what we want, of not having our expectations met, often triggers our most painful and unhealed emotions. Whether we feel hurt, angry, or anxious, these very reactions are telling us where we're most stuck; they're also pointing to exactly what we need to work with. So whether we withdraw or attack, whether we blame or mollify, whether we self-justify or self-blame, we're still caught in trying to fix the external situation in order to avoid feeling our emotional pain. We're also missing out on the real healing response, which is to understand and stay with our *own* experience.

One very helpful tool in both clarifying and working with our relationship difficulties is to return to the three questions: Am I truly happy right now? What blocks happiness? Can I surrender to what is? There are some applicable examples of how this process works in chapter 6, but basically, the first question helps identify what we're actually feeling (often we don't know). The second question shows us where we're stuck in our conditioning—our expectations, demands, or unhealed pain. Once we see our expectations clearly, and once we work through our surface emotional reactions, we usually reach that uncomfortable place where we begin to feel our deepest fears—such as the fear of being unworthy, the fear of being alone, the fear of being hurt again, the fear of rejection, or the fear of the loss of control or safety. Our fears may not necessarily be logical, but we still believe at our core that they are the truth, and they certainly dictate how we feel and how we live, thus blocking any chance for true contentment.

Finally, the third question leads us directly into the experiential process of coming face to face with our own fears—the fears that are almost always at the root of our unhappiness in relationships. Asking the third question—Can I surrender to what is?—allows us to do the one thing that can help free us from the domination of our fears: that is, to welcome them in and actually *feel* them. We may *think* we can't stand to feel our fears, but the truth is we just don't want to, primarily because they feel so uncomfortable. But over time we can develop the courage and confidence to stay present with our fears. We learn again and again that it's awareness that heals; and gradually, the fears, which at one point felt so solid and unapproachable, are now much more workable.

As we become more inwardly free from our conditioning and our fears, the love and connection that are possible in relationships tend to flow through us more naturally. As our defenses are lowered, our heart opens, and there is a natural desire to give from the generosity of the heart. We discover that genuine happiness in relationships is not a product of having our expectations met or getting what we want but rather it is the consequence of freely giving in order to bring happiness to another. Nearly every parent has experienced this at some point—their deepest joy coming from giving unselfishly to their children. Unfortunately, this truth is often forgotten as relationships become more complex, and especially as fear supersedes our innate desire to give from the heart.

But again, as we work with our conditioning and fear, giving becomes our natural response. I had a student who was struggling mightily with jealousy and possessiveness around his wife's friendliness with other men. She wasn't having affairs or making overtures toward them; she was just very outgoing and genuinely interested in others. But her friendliness nonetheless provoked his deepest fears. When he tried to curb her behavior it proved to be counterproductive, in that she became resentful of being controlled. But as he looked more deeply into his reactions, and slowly learned to welcome and reside in his deeply seated fear of not being enough, he gradually became free of the dark cloud of fear. He was then able to give his wife the freedom to be herself. This giving did not come from a "should"—it was the natural response of the generosity of the heart. However, he was only able to access this generosity, and ultimately his own genuine happiness, by first clearly seeing his own agendas and deep fears and then fully residing in them, no matter how unwanted or unpleasant.

Working with the fears that block our natural tendency to give is key. Years ago I met a hospice patient who appeared to be very reserved; in fact, he was almost unfriendly. I had been cautioned by the hospice coordinator that this patient was very angry and prone to holler at people, but I was willing to see how it played out. Although I didn't expect to change him, in retrospect, I see I did have the expectation that if I was friendly to him, he would be friendly in return. However, my friendliness didn't seem to impact him at all—he remained reserved and almost aloof. My reaction was quite predictable—old conditioning tends to come up rapidly when certain buttons are pushed. In this case, his behavior provoked two of my deeper fears: the fear of not measuring up and the fear of being unappreciated.

Fortunately, it was very clear to me what was going on, and instead of trying harder to be friendly and get what I wanted, which was his acceptance and a sense of control, I let myself fully feel the experience of fear. As I welcomed it in, and breathed the sensations of fear right into the center of the chest, something remarkable happened: I was no longer concerned about how he felt toward me. Instead I felt genuine empathy for the prison he was trapped in—feeling so defended and held back. So the next time I visited him, I no longer tried to be friendly as a way to manipulate him; rather, my natural friendliness came from the genuine wish that he be free from his suffering. Once I was no longer caught in my own fears, it was the most natural thing to give to him from the heart; and although he didn't change drastically in the short time he had left before he died, he definitely was able to drop his defensiveness and extend the warmth of his own heart as best as he could.

Learning to see our own expectations clearly, and then working with the fears that drive us, is one way to cultivate our innate capacity to give in relationships. But we don't have to wait for the heart to be free from fear before we give ourselves to another. We can also practice *intentional giving*, in part as a means of working directly with whatever blocks the natural generosity of the heart. When we give to another even when the desire to give is not present, it will no doubt highlight our resistance and give us the opportunity to work with whatever specifically blocks access to the open heart. In giving intentionally we are not acting out of a mental ideal or a "should." We are acting from the understanding that the act of giving can help encourage us to work with what we need to address within ourselves.

For example, if we have difficulty listening to our partner, we may decide to make a sincere effort to intentionally give the gift of truly listening. But it's not so easy to just decide to listen and have it happen automatically. To truly listen to another requires dropping our Me—our impatience and boredom and our need to be right. It means we have to stop formulating our opinions while the other person is talking, and instead be open to what someone is saying and feeling. Dropping the Me is especially difficult if we've grown accustomed to loving the drama—making Me the center of the story.

Yet, as we try to listen intentionally, we can also stay aware of breathing into the chest center—which keeps us physically centered rather than caught in the self-centered mind of Me. We can learn to ask the other person questions to help clarify what is being said, and through our efforts to work through our resistance, over time we can discover that it's possible to begin to naturally give the gift of truly listening—and even be as interested in another as we are in ourselves.

This is just one example of intentional giving. Another would be to practice speaking more openly and honestly, particularly if we tend to hold a lot back. Sometimes, however, our desire to be honest and bare our soul might go too far. For example, a man went into the confession booth and said to the priest, "I'm seventy-five years old and I slept with two beautiful twenty-one-year-old women last night." The priest asked, "When did you last come to confession?" The man said, "I've never been to confession. I'm Jewish." The priest asked, "Then why are you telling me this?" The man emphatically replied, "I'm telling *everybody*!"

This humorous example is benign and a bit exaggerated, but in most cases, giving our honesty to another doesn't mean we say *everything* we think and feel. First, we need to be honest and clear within ourselves. Then, our words can be tempered with the questions Buddha raised about communication: Is it timely? Is it necessary? Is it kind?

Of course, there can't be a simplistic formula for any of

this, because life is messy, complicated, and unpredictable. But the point of giving intentionally is to push us to work with our own fears, and the unskillfulness that comes out of them. This is particularly true when we attempt to give to others that which they most want yet we're most unwilling to give. To better understand how this dynamic might play out, think of someone close to you; ask what that person might want from you that you feel a definite resistance to giving. I'm talking about something that you have the capacity to give, but not the willingness. If you reflect on your own example, you might see how the intentional act of giving could very well push you to confront the exact place where you're most stuck.

If we're willing to take the step of intentionally giving even when our insides are saying "no," it becomes an opportunity to work with the layers of anger and fear that are keeping us stuck. Once we directly face our own fears, it's possible to experience the freedom of giving up our "self"—that is, giving up wanting things our own way, wanting control, wanting to be right. Ultimately, we can experience the genuine happiness that comes from giving naturally from the heart, rather than being controlled by our fears.

For example, if our partner is very sensitive to criticism, we may make the decision to give nonjudgment, which means we make the effort to withhold verbal (and even nonverbal) judgments and criticisms. In doing so, in giving up our demands of how the other should be, we are forced to face the fear of not getting what we want. Another example could be the person who fears chaos. In this case, we might decide to give our partner control over household planning and finances. In intentionally giving our partner the independence they truly want, we are also pushing ourselves to face our fear of imagined chaos or lack of control. In facing our fears directly, we also have the possibility of moving from giving intentionally, as a task, to giving naturally from the unobstructed heart.

A Day of Nonjudgment

To see the value of the practice of intentional giving, try the following exercise. Pick someone that you have a lot of judgments about, preferably someone with whom you have frequent contact. Then, one day per week, from the time you wake up until the time you go to bed, withhold all judgments and criticisms of the other person, especially the judgments that have the strongest emotional charge. This means refraining from indulging in these critical thoughts and feelings. In other words, whenever the judgments arise, notice them, but don't solidify them by replaying them or speaking them. Instead, just try to experience the physical tension in the body that is the result of holding these beliefs.

The point of this exercise isn't to change your behavior or to suppress your emotions. It's designed to allow you to face yourself. In giving nonjudgment to another, which is what everyone wants and also one of the hardest things to give, we're actually giving *ourselves* a great gift. This gift is the opportunity to see that *our judgments and criticisms are always more about us than they are about the other person.* This understanding gives us the matrix to work more easily and directly with our deepest fears and attachments. But beware that it may take several weeks or more of doing this exercise to see its real value.

Concluding Thoughts

Giving from the heart in our relationships involves being willing to work with our fears, which ultimately requires that we give up our sense of entitlement—the belief that relationships should be easy and pleasant or that the other person should be able to take away our discomfort. This entitlement is one of the major barriers to happiness, because until we see through it, we will not be willing to take responsibility for our own fears—the very fears that block genuine connectedness. Until we realize the necessity of facing our fears, we will remain disconnected from ourselves, and, consequently, we'll remain disconnected from others. This means that our relationships will rarely be satisfying, except on a superficial level. But as we befriend our fears—no longer fearing them—we can begin to experience real intimacy with others. This is the true ground for the love and happiness that are possible in relationships.

When the deeper happiness of true contentment replaces the power struggles—the blaming, the needing to be right, the fear-based protections—relationships can serve as a conduit through which love flows naturally. Giving is no longer a chore; it becomes the natural expression of the generosity of the heart. This is the point in relationships when even our mundane daily interactions can be imbued with the genuine happiness of connection. We don't have to be doing special things or making special efforts, yet all of the little routines of a shared life can take on a richer quality. This sense of ease and appreciation feels quite natural, but unfortunately, it doesn't come to us naturally. Rather, it is the result of our ongoing practice—of learning to reside in the present moment, cultivating appreciation and loving-kindness, and learning how to give intentionally, including working with whatever arises to block our efforts to give.

As our practice matures, many small moments in our day become portals into the inner delight of just being with another. For example, sometimes when my wife Elizabeth smiles, which she does frequently, it serves as a reflection of, a reminder of, the shining quality of her true nature, of the true nature of being human; and when I experience that, it is not hard to tap into the genuine happiness that is the natural state of our unobstructed being. The point is, when we no longer relate primarily from our self-centered motivation to have life be the way we want it to be, our relationships can become one of the most fruitful paths to the depth of happiness that we're all looking for. We can discover the simple but profound truth that love is not about having someone else make us happy; love is about wanting *them* to be happy.

14

Forgiveness

Perhaps one of the commonest places we get stuck, and consequently one of the places that most prevents happiness, is in holding onto resentments. If there is even one person that we can't forgive, it closes our hearts in bitterness and will prevent us from experiencing the equanimity of genuine happiness.

Forgiveness is actually an inherent quality of the awakened heart. Unfortunately, it doesn't come to us naturally; it is hard work! Consider how tenaciously we hold on to being right when we feel that someone has done us wrong, even when that stance obviously brings us unhappiness. During my first marriage, my former wife and I got into a typical power struggle, where we both dug in and held on to our grudges. Even after our divorce I found it hard to give up my resentments, and although we maintained a friendly relationship, there was often a little edge to our conversations.

However, when it became obvious to me that in holding on to my resentments I was really hurting myself, I started doing a forgiveness meditation. What amazed me was how much resistance there was to even entertaining the idea of forgiving her. Part of the meditation was to picture her and try to breathe her image into the heart area, but each time I tried, I was met with a visceral "no"—as if pushing her away.

Fortunately, the meditation was structured to allow for this resistance; the instruction was to stay present with the physical feeling of "no," rather than trying to jump over it.

Over time, as the resistance softened, I was able to feel the layers of anger and hurt—emotions that were the direct result of the expectations that were present when I entered into the relationship. In fact, these were expectations I wasn't even aware of at the time, and when they weren't met, I felt betrayed, resentful, and bitter. I also believed strongly that my reactions were justified. Yet, as I became more aware of the story line of beliefs and emotions that held my resentments in place, and as I was able to stay with my own pain without blaming her for it, the dark cloud began to lift. At that point it was easier to breathe her image into the heart area and also to extend forgiveness, because it was so clear that she never intended to hurt me. When I could see clearly that the resentment and the power struggle arose from our mutual blindness and hurt, forgiveness came forth naturally.

Although it took us many years of fumbling and stumbling to get to this place, in the end we were both able give up our resentments completely. By the time she died a few years ago we had come to truly love each other as friends, something that would never have been possible if we hadn't learned what it takes to truly forgive one another.

I heard the Buddhist teacher Jack Kornfield tell a story about a golfer who was awarded a check for winning a tournament, and when he was walking to the parking lot a woman came up to him and told him a heart-wrenching story about her sick child. She told him that if the child didn't get help soon, he would die. The golfer promptly signed his check over to the woman. A month later one of the golfer's buddies told him that he heard about what happened in the parking lot and that he also heard that the woman was a con artist and didn't even have a sick child. The golfer replied, "That's the best news I've heard in a long time—a child isn't going to die."

The golfer obviously did not get caught in the fear of betrayal that would have led him to feel mistreated, and to consequently harbor resentment toward the woman. If he had taken the path of bitterness, no doubt many people would have agreed with him. But instead, he was able to listen to the voice of the heart, the heart that is naturally concerned with the welfare of others, rather than the hard-hearted habit of holding grudges.

It may be easy for us to be kind, and also forgiving, when life is going well. But it's only when life gets difficult that the depth of our spiritual practice is revealed. *For our kindness to be real, it can't depend on how others treat us,* or on how we feel at any given moment. Truthfully, when we feel mistreated, kindness is often the farthest thing from our minds and hearts. Yet, for genuine happiness to be possible, we ultimately have to go to that deep place within us where true kindness and forgiveness can be accessed. This means we must attend to whatever blocks access to our hearts.

One of the most important things I've learned from the forgiveness practice is to never underestimate how hard it is to give up our resentments. Even when we see how much the resentment is hurting us by keeping our heart closed, we can hold onto it with a stubbornness that defies common sense. Fortunately, part of the practice of forgiveness, and part of the path toward genuine happiness, is to first acknowledge whatever blocks the path. We start where we are, not where we think we should be. Now, when I teach the forgiveness practice to students, I try to emphasize how important it is to acknowledge the resistance, and to stay present with the physical experience of it for as long as it takes. When we do this we can learn a great deal about ourselves.

What makes forgiveness so difficult? Part of it has to do with the complexity of what happens when someone says or does something that hurts us. We often react not only to the incident that just happened but perhaps more so to the well of past pain that is stirred up in the moment, because feeling hurt often taps into the deepest layers of our own conditioning. This can trigger feelings of worthlessness or powerlessness, and it is quite natural that our defense system will want to attack back, so that we don't have to experience the vulnerability of these painful feelings. When that happens, what we usually do is blame the other. We insist on being right, on elevating ourselves by putting the other down. But in doing so, we place a protective armoring around the heart; and as we feed our anger through blaming, it slowly turns into resentment and bitterness.

The saddest part of this whole dynamic is that in falling into the syndrome of anger, blame, and resentment, we become disconnected from our own hearts. When we hold onto bitterness, our lives become very small and narrow, and we are destined to experience the ongoing unhappiness of living from a closed heart. There's an old Hebrew proverb: "When you live to seek revenge you dig two graves." Allowing our lives to close down in resentment hurts ourselves as well as others. This is why the first step in the forgiveness practice is to feel the remorse of going against our own heart, our own true nature. At some point we develop the understanding that by holding onto our resentment we are hurting ourselves, perhaps even more than the other person is hurting us. This understanding can become a pivotal turning point whereby we can actually engage in the process of forgiveness.

Once, when I was attacked verbally in public by someone I knew well, my first response was intense anger, quickly followed by judgments and blame. It was easy to focus on the shortcomings of the person who attacked me, and it was also easy to use his behavior to justify my anger and to elevate myself in self-righteousness. Fortunately, I sensed that something about my response was off. It quickly became clear that my anger and resentment were a way of avoiding having to actually feel the part that was most painful—feeling hurt and betrayed. It also gradually became clear that in taking the path of anger and resentment I was choosing to cut myself off from my own heart, and certainly from the other person. As easy as it was to blame him for my emotional distress, the truth was that in indulging my anger and righteous defensiveness I had lost my *own* way.

These intense, turbulent experiences are the times when the practice of forgiveness is most needed; these are also the times when forgiveness is most difficult to access. For me, in the situation mentioned above, once I experienced the remorse of choosing the dark path of resentment, the first step was to refrain from blaming. Every time my mind began making a case by putting him down, I literally told myself, *"Don't go there!"* Instead, I tried to stay with the intense physical experience in the body—the feelings of heat, contraction, and dis-ease. By residing in, and surrendering to, the present-moment experience of anger, the solidity of the feelings began to diminish somewhat. But they didn't just go away. Even after all my years of practice, something in me was still fighting to hold onto resentment.

That's when I started doing the forgiveness meditation—trying to breathe the image of the friend who had turned against me into the heart. At first there was a lot of resistance—the mind still wanted to focus on the other person's faults and on how I had been mistreated. But as the resistance gradually softened, other feelings that were somewhat below the surface began to rise. First there was the layer of hurt, followed by the experience of grief and loss. Then there was the fear of powerlessness, and the still deeper and even more powerful fear of disconnection. As I rested in these experiences—breathing the physical sensations right into the center of the chest—I gradually experienced the healing power of the heart. Eventually I could silently and sincerely say to my friend, "I forgive you."

Through the forgiveness practice it became vividly clear to me that by choosing the path of blame and resentment I was hurting myself much more than my friend had; and that the suffering was ongoing, being relived on a regular basis. It also became clear that his actions had no doubt come from his own pain, and that perhaps I had had some part in that. It's important to understand that none of this was intellectual justification or analysis—it all came directly from the willingness to reside in and experience my own distress; and when I got to the place where I experienced real forgiveness, it was very easy to feel compassion for my friend and to naturally wish him well.

This incident happened several years ago, and since that time, whenever little feelings of resentment pop up, I ask myself the three questions. With the first question—Am I truly happy right now?—it's so easy to see that as long as I entertain even a sliver of resentment, I will not be able to experience genuine happiness. With the second question—What blocks happiness?—it has become obvious that indulging in blame is one of the major obstructions to both happiness and love. And with the third question—Can I surrender to what is?—I have found time and again that one of the keys to true contentment is the ability to simply stay present with exactly what we are experiencing right now, minus our thoughts and judgments about it; that is, feeling into the bodily sensations, and refraining from indulging the thoughts about the person or incident.

We may not need to engage in an intense forgiveness practice very often, but as long as we are caught in resentment, however small, our ability to live from the deeper happiness of equanimity will be blocked. The practice of forgiveness guides us directly through that blockage, allowing us to address the emotional pain out of which our resentment arises. More than anything, the practice of forgiveness allows us to reconnect with our own hearts; but the only way to actually engage in a forgiveness practice is to persevere, coming back to our experience again and again, letting layer after layer of anger and fear fall away in the process.

FORGIVENESS MEDITATION

STEP ONE—REMORSE

See if you can get in touch with the remorse of going against your own heart—that by holding onto resentment you are hurting yourself more than the other person is hurting you.

STEP TWO—RESISTANCE

Picture the person you feel resentment toward and try to breathe their image into the area in the center of the chest. If you feel resistance, don't try to force it; just stay with the *physical experience of resistance* as long as it takes for the resistance to soften. This might take numerous occasions of doing the forgiveness meditation for this softening to begin to happen.

STEP THREE—SURRENDER

Ask yourself: Can I surrender to what is? Whatever you are feeling—whether it is hurt, anger, resentment, bitterness, or fear—try to stay with the *physical experience* of the emotion. Label any strong thoughts that arise, but keep coming back to the body over and over. Gradually try to breathe the painful feelings into the center of the chest on the inbreath, until they can rest there without struggle. This step may also take a fair number of practice sessions.

STEP FOUR—FORGIVENESS

Silently say the words of forgiveness.

[Say the person's name],
I forgive you.

I forgive you for what you have done,
Whether intentionally or unintentionally,
From which I experienced pain.

I forgive you,
Because I know that what you did
Came from your own pain.

Return to this meditation as many times as you need to until the words of forgiveness come forth naturally from the heart. At that time, the words are no longer tools to help nurture forgiveness—they are simply a verbal expression of your genuine openhearted compassion.

Final Words
Beyond the Myth of Happiness

Let's go back to the beginning by again asking the question: What is this elusive thing called happiness? Personal happiness is the good feeling that comes when we experience pleasure or get what we want. The deeper, more genuine experience of happiness is the natural state of our Being when we are not so caught up in our self-centered thoughts and emotions. It is the experience of true contentment, of being fundamentally okay with our life as it is, no longer so attached to getting what the small mind of ego wants, nor demanding that life be a particular way.

Personal happiness is based on a myth: the myth tells us that we'll be happy if we get what we want—the right job, the right mate, the right body, etc. This may be true in the very short term, but happiness based on externals will rarely survive life's inevitable blows. The corollary of the happiness myth is equally untrue—that we can't be happy if we get what we *don't* want, namely discomfort in any form. Yet, as many who have suffered serious illness have found out, it is possible to experience genuine equanimity even in the midst of prolonged discomfort.

As long as we chase the myth, trying to get happiness by attempting to manipulate and control life—whether through trying harder to succeed, trying to please others, seeking comfort and diversions, or even using spiritual practice to become calm—we will continue to trap ourselves on the roller coaster cycle of personal happiness and unhappiness. And sadly, we may never taste the true contentment that comes when we learn how to stay present with what is, exactly as it is.

Staying present is not so easy, but one very effective tool to guide us is to ask the three questions. The first question—Am I truly happy right now?—allows us to recognize our state of mind, something we're ordinarily only vaguely aware of. The second question—What blocks happiness?—guides us to look more specifically at where we're stuck, such as in self-judgments, blaming, anger, or fear. Unless we see clearly what's actually going on we won't be able to effectively address what blocks happiness. The third question—Can I surrender to what is?—is key; it reminds us to welcome our experience, however difficult, as our path to freedom. It also directs us to reside in exactly what we are experiencing right now, minus our usual thought-based melodrama.

Staying present—residing in, or surrendering into, the physical reality of the present moment—may not sound very exciting or enticing. But staying present with what is gradually allows us to see through the seeming solidity of our self-imposed boundaries—our sense of entitlement, our beliefs and judgments, our deeply held emotions and patterns of behavior. As the solidity of the narrow self-centered world of I-as-a-Me becomes more porous, we can live increasingly from a vaster sense of who we are and what life is.

The purpose of human life is not to be happy, although we certainly all want that; the purpose of human life is to awaken to who we truly are. The more we are in touch with who we really are, the closer we are to living from genuine happiness. As we learn to reside in our present-moment experience, we gradually discover that our true nature of connectedness is without bounds. The only reason we create the limited world of beliefs and conditioned behaviors is to make sense of things and survive. Yet when we remain solely in this bounded world, we are cut off from the mystery of our Being, as well as from the true contentment of living from the open-heartedness that is our true nature.

From this place of connectedness our deepest aspiration is to give from the natural generosity of the heart. Although there is no "secret" to living a genuinely happy life, the deepest happiness of equanimity grows with our ability to stay with present-moment reality, and flowers as we water the roots of the generosity of the heart—including our inherent capacity for gratitude, loving-kindness, and forgiveness.

As we see what blocks genuine happiness, we discover what we have to give up so that our natural happiness can come forth. When we give up the busyness of the thinking mind and reside in the physical reality of the present moment, we can experience the equanimity of being at home with ourselves. When we give up our entitlement, we can experience a genuine appreciation and gratitude for life. When we give up our judgments, especially our self-judgments, we can experience the openhearted friendliness of loving-kindness. And when we give up our resentments, we can experience the lightness of heart that comes with genuine forgiveness.

More than anything, we have to give up the myth about happiness—that we deserve to be happy, as if it's our birthright; that we will be happy if we get what we want; that we can't be happy if we're in discomfort. Once we are free of this illusion, the path is much more straightforward. With a combination of courage and curiosity, we can persevere with the blue-collar work of practice: the mundane, everyday effort of coming back again and again to staying present with exactly what we are experiencing right now. And although we need to have the serious intention to persevere, we don't need to be somber. Humor is always a good counterbalance, as is the quality of loving-kindness. Both humor and loving-kindness temper our grim tendency to judge ourselves as lacking.

Sometimes it may be hard to believe that true contentment is even possible. That's because we've gotten so good at what we practice, which is pursuing the myth of happiness and at the same time doing all the things that perpetuate our un-happiness. But we can also get good at practicing something different, namely living in a more genuine way. I don't want to pretend that it's easy to cultivate presence, or to learn to live from the natural generosity of the heart, but I can say unequivocally that it *is* possible. The wonderful thing is, when we can finally give up our self-centered pursuit of trying to get what we want, we let go of a very heavy burden that we've been carrying around our whole lives, and the lightness of heart we experience feels natural instead of forced. This is the essence of true contentment. Only at this point can we understand and live from Zen's classical and timeless invita-tion: Appreciate this precious life!

About the Author

Ezra Bayda lives and teaches at the Zen Center of San Diego. He is the author of *Being Zen, At Home in the Muddy Water, Saying Yes to Life (Even the Hard Parts),* and *Zen Heart.*

Initially trained in the Gurdjieff tradition, Ezra has practiced Zen meditation since 1970 and has been teaching Zen since 1995. He is also the founder of the Santa Rosa Zen Group in Santa Rosa, California.

For more information, please visit www.zencentersandiego .org.

Also by Ezra Bayda

Being Zen: Bringing Meditation to Life (Shambhala, 2002)

We can use whatever life presents, Ezra Bayda teaches, to strengthen our spiritual practice—including the turmoil of daily life. What we need is the willingness to just be with our experiences—whether they are painful or pleasing—opening ourselves to the reality of our lives without trying to fix or change anything. But doing this requires that we confront our most deeply rooted fears and assumptions in order to gradually become free of the constrictions and suffering they create. Then we can awaken to the loving-kindness that is at the heart of our being.

At Home in the Muddy Water: A Guide to Finding Peace within Everyday Chaos (Shambhala, 2004)

In this book, Bayda applies the simple Zen teaching of being "at home in the muddy water" to a range of everyday concerns—including relationships, trust, sexuality, and money—showing that everything we need to practice is right here before us, and that peace and fulfillment is available to everyone, right here, right now, no matter what their circumstances.

Saying Yes to Life (Even the Hard Parts) (Wisdom, 2005)

The teachings in *Saying Yes to Life* are presented in the form of brief aphorisms and one-page essays. Told in simple language, they provide inspiration for each day by stressing the importance of drawing meaning from life's paradoxes—opening to the unwanted, recognizing the possibility of equanimity within difficulty, and living for now rather than later.

Zen Heart: Simple Advice for Living with Mindfulness and Compassion (Shambhala, 2008)

There's a secret to spiritual practice, and it's surprisingly simple: learn to be present with attention. Do that, and the whole world becomes your teacher, you wake up to the sacredness of every aspect of existence, and compassion for others arises without even thinking about it. It's indeed just that simple, says Ezra Bayda, but that doesn't necessarily mean it's easy—especially when being present brings us up against the painful parts of life. Bayda provides a wealth of practical advice for making difficult experiences a valued part of the path and for making mindulness a daily habit.